KYONGJU, Old Capital of Shilla Dynasty Enlivened with 2000-year History

- Plan/Kim, Young-Joo
- Photography/Kim, Chnn-Myong
  Kim, Young-Joo
  Choi, Won-Oh
- Writing/Kim, Young-Joo
- English Translation/Kwon, Bo-Taig
- Edition/Kim, Young-Joo

Published by Kim, Yong-Soo
Address/2F, Song Hyun Bldg, Youngdungpo-8ga,
Youngdungpo-Gu, Seoul, Korea. 150-083
Tel/631-7334～4, Fax/631-7335
Duly registered 17 February, 1995
Registration No. 13-603

Price ₩ 6,000

CONTENTS

History of Kyŏngju

Shilla Era

B.C. 57	Six founding villages of Shilla were under the kingship of Park, Hyŏkkŏse.
A.D. 417-458	Introductionof Buddhism in the 19th King Nulji.
A.D. 528	Construction of Pulguksa Temple during the reign of 15th year of the King Pŏp'ŭng, the 23rd King of Shilla.
A.D. 553	Completion of Hwangryongsa Temple in 14th year of the 24th king of Shilla, Chinhŭng after 90 years of beginning.
A.D. 634	Construction of Punhwangsa Temple in the 3rd year of the 27th Queen Sŏndŏk.
A.D. 632-647	Construction of Ch'ŏmsŏngdae Observatory during the reign of the 27th Queen Sŏndŏk.
A.D. 674	Construction of Anapji in the 14th year of the 30th king Munmu.
A.D. 676	Completion of Unification, by finally expelling T'ang troops in the 16th year of the 30th king, Munmu.
A.D. 751	Construction of Sŏkkuram in the 10th year of the 35th king, Kyŏngdŏk.
A.D. 771	Cast of the Mystery Bell of the King Sŏndŏk, the 7th year of the 36th King, Hyegong.
A.D. 927	Invasion of the chief of Post-Paekche, Kyŏnhwon, in the 4th year of the 55th king, Kyŏngae.
A.D. 935	Downfall of Shilla, in the 9th year of the 56th king Kyŏngsun.

Koryŏ Era

A.D. 935	Annexed to Koryŏ and renamed as Kyŏngju, in the 18th year of the founder-king of Koryŏ.
A.D. 1002	Renamed as Andongkimju-daedohobu in the 5th year of the 6th king of Koryŏ, Mokchong.
A.D. 1030	Establishment of Tongkyŏng, in the 21st year of the 8th king, Hyŏnjong.
A.D. 1238	Burning-up of Hwangryongsa Temple during the Mongol Invasion, in the 25th year of the 23rd king, Kojong.
A.D. 1308	Renamed as Kyerimbu with Puyun as ruler, in the 34th year of the 25th king, Ch'ungryŏl.
A.D. 1326	Ruled by Anryŏmsa, in the 13th year of the 27th king, Ch'ungsuk.

Lee Dynasty Era

A.D. 1408	Deprived of Kyŏngsang-do Office, with only Left and Right Divisions of Troops left, in the 8th year of the 3rd king of Lee Dynasty, T'aejong.
A.D. 1413	Kyerimbu was renamed as Kyŏngjubu in the 13th year of the 3rd king T'aejong.
A.D. 1519	Kyŏngsang-do was divided into two: Left and right, in the 14th year of the 11th king, Chungjong. Office of left Kyŏngsang-do lay in Kyŏngjubu.
A.D. 1593	Burning-up of Pulguksa Temple in the 26th year of the 14th king, Sŏnjo, During the Japanese Invasion.
A.D. 1593	Left and Right Kyŏngsang-do's were unified, with the office laid in Sangju, in the 26th year of the 14th king Sŏnjo.
A.D. 1659	Partly restoration of Pulguksa Temple, in the 10th year of the 17th king, Hyojong.
A.D. 1859	Renamed as Kyŏngjubu, in the 32nd year of the 26th king, Kojong.

Modern Era

A.D. 1914	Entitled as a ''myŏn''
A.D. 1931	Entitled as an ''eub''
A.D. 1955	Entitled as a ''city''
A.D. 1971	Establishment of ten-year comprehensive Tourism Development Plan.
A.D. 1973	Restoration of Pulguksa Temple
A.D. 1976	Establishment of Daenŭngwon Park and maintenance of Historic Sites.
A.D. 1979	Construction of Pomun Tourism Complex.
A.D. 1980	Restoration of Anapchi.
A.D. 1983	Establishment of 5-year comprehensive Tourism Development.

Of many eastern countries, Kyŏngju is the very place where the sunshine reaches first and here, from the son of heaven and founding father of Shilla, Pak Hyŏk-Kŏ-Se Kŏsŏgan through the 56th King Kyŏngsun, 992-year Shilla culture was blossomed.

At about the same time that Koguryŏ and Paekche established themselves as ancient kingdoms and reached the peak in their power, Shilla belatedly formed six founding villages into a state on the basis of the tribe of Saro, one of 12 small countries located in Chinhan.

But Shilla conquered the two developed states, Koguryŏ and Paekche to unify them into one.

Achieving unification, Shilla absorbed and amalgamated their culture. Especially, actively receiving the brilliant culture of Tang Dynasty, Shilla built up its unique culture,

Kyŏngju, Old Capital of Shilla Dynasty Enlivened with 2000-Year History

which resulted in the golden age of Shilla culture.

After official approval of Buddhism with the martyrdom of Lee Ch'a-don, Buddhism became prosperous. In the meantime, such learned monk as Paedŏk appeared to educate people in spiritual aspect, so they erected temples, large and small, pagodas and Buddha's statues to achieve resplendent Buddhist culture.

Granite of good quality scattered everywhere enabled people in Shilla to be accustomed to masonry rather early. As a result, they left excellent stone structure behind and they embossed many Buddha-to-be's on the rocks of mountains to build up the Paradise they wanted.

Not only Buddhist statue or things made of stone, but also those of gold, gift bronze and iron were developed, and with them ingenious metal processing skill was developed.

Such cultural heritage depended not only on the skill of then artisan but also on the sound and ambitious mentality of the people in Shilla, dextrous skill trained in ordinary times and thorough aesthetic sense. Such factors were united into wealthy power, which made possible the formation of our original culture with everlasting light and beauty.

At the turn of the 9th century, Shilla's national strength began to decline and the cultural heritage achieved at that time lost its bold and vigorous strength it had had at the time of unification.

Like this, Shilla, though it was the last of the three countries, conquered the two developed ones to unify and it did not transfer the capital of Kyŏngju until it died out.

Such fact became the very generative power for Shilla to form the strong basis and served as a momentum for many remaining relics and heritages, so Kyŏngju is dotted with many cultural heritages to the extent that it deserves the name of open museum.

Going through the millennium of Shilla and another millennium, Kyŏngju is full of rocks, large and small, streets, and valleys filled with various legends and touch of Shilla people.

Thanks to its preserved civilization of two thousand years which is not common elsewhere, Kyŏngju was named, by UNESCO in 1979, one of the world's ten historic sites.

Like this, Kyŏngju is not only an old cultural capital but also a cultural heritage important enough to be named a world's historic site.

Brilliant and Majestic Pulguksa

– Historic Site and Scenic Beauty No. 1 –

▼ Panorama of Pulguksa Temple, beautiful and magnificant, tinged with autumnal tints.

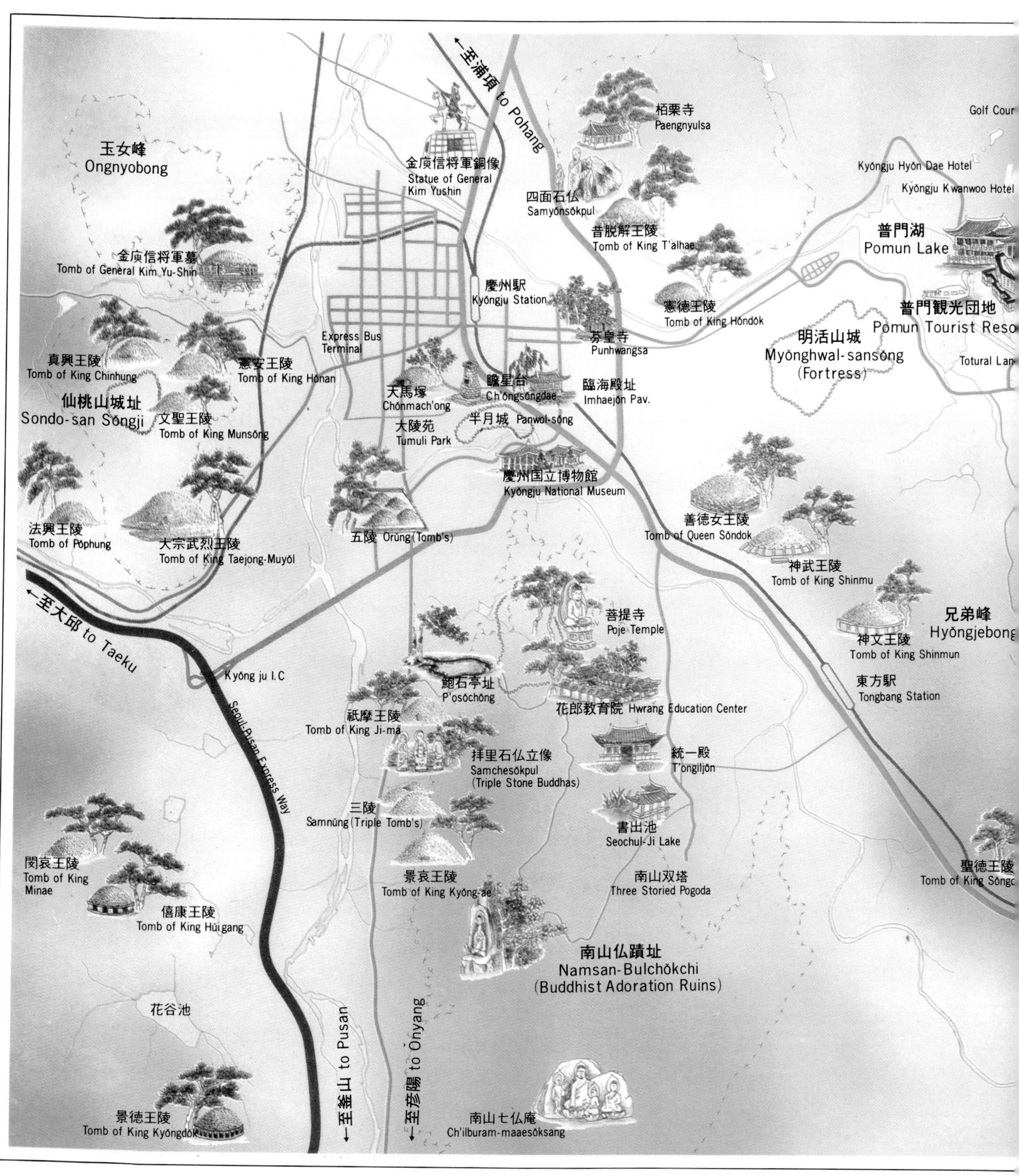

←至浦項 to Pohang
金庾信将軍銅像
Statue of General Kim Yushin
栢栗寺
Paengnyulsa
Golf Cour
Kyŏngju Hyŏn Dae Hotel
Kyŏngju Kwanwoo Hotel
玉女峰
Ongnyobong
四面石仏
Samyŏnsŏkpul
昔脱解王陵
Tomb of King T'alhae
普門湖
Pomun Lake
金庾信将軍墓
Tomb of General Kim Yu-Shin
慶州駅
Kyŏngju Station
憲徳王陵
Tomb of King Hŏndŏk
普門観光団地
Pomun Tourist Reso
芬皇寺
Punhwangsa
明活山城
Myŏnghwal-sansŏng
(Fortress)
Express Bus Terminal
真興王陵
Tomb of King Chinhung
憲安王陵
Tomb of King Hŏnan
Totural Lan
天馬塚
Chŏnmach'ong
瞻星台
Ch'ŏngsŏngdae
臨海殿址
Imhaejŏn Pav.
仙桃山城址
Sondo-san Sŏngji
文聖王陵
Tomb of King Munsŏng
大陵苑
Tumuli Park
半月城 Panwol-sŏng
慶州国立博物館
Kyŏngju National Museum
善徳女王陵
Tomb of Queen Sŏndok
法興王陵
Tomb of Pŏphung
大宗武烈王陵
Tomb of King Taejong-Muyŏl
五陵 Orŭng (Tomb's)
神武王陵
Tomb of King Shinmu
←至大邱 to Taeku
菩提寺
Poje Temple
兄弟峰
Hyŏngjebong
神文王陵
Tomb of King Shinmun
Kyŏng ju I.C
鮑石亭址
P'osŏchŏng
東方駅
Tongbang Station
Seoul-Pusan Express Way
花郎教育院 Hwrang Education Center
祇摩王陵
Tomb of King Ji-ma
拝里石仏立像
Samchesŏkpul
(Triple Stone Buddhas)
統一殿
T'ongiljŏn
三陵
Samnŭng (Triple Tomb's)
書出池
Seochul-Ji Lake
閔哀王陵
Tomb of King Minae
景哀王陵
Tomb of King Kyŏng-ae
南山双塔
Three Storied Pogoda
聖徳王陵
Tomb of King Sŏngo
僖康王陵
Tomb of King Hŭigang
南山仏蹟址
Namsan-Bulchŏkchi
(Buddhist Adoration Ruins)
花谷池
←至釜山 to Pusan
←至彦陽 to Ŏnyang
景徳王陵
Tomb of King Kyŏngdŏk
南山七仏庵
Ch'ilburam-maaesŏksang

The syllables Pulguk in the word Pulguksa mean the Land of Happiness and they show the aspiration for a country with no lack in anything, no agony and no pain.

This temple, built in the 15th year of 23rd king Pŏphŭng (528), was called Hwaŏmbulguksa or Pŏbryusa. It was reset to work by the prime minister Kim, Dae-sŏng in the 10th year of 35th king Kyŏngdŏk (751) and through 17-year construction, it was rebuilt in the 36th King Hyegong (774) and since then it was called Pulguksa.

At the time of its completion, it was a very big temple comprising 80 wooden buildings and two great monks P'yohun and Shinrim were invited to stay there. Going through Koryŏ and Chosŏn Dynasties, however, it contracted and barely kept itself in existence and by the fire in Imjinwaeran, Japanese Invasion, in the 14th king Sŏnjo (1593) all wooden buildings were burnt up 819 years after its first complete construction.

After that, it was reconstructed little by little, but it was impossible to resume its old brilliant image. Then, from 1969 to 1973 the construction site was excavated and on the basis of the excavation, it was rebuilt on a large scale to take on the present image.

▼ Vernal view of the frontage with two stone bridges Ch'ilbo — Yŏnhwa and Ch'ŏngun — Paegun connecting secular world to Buddhist one.

To get to the precinct of Pulguksa, we should pass Iljumun which has a line of columns and a hanging board with the calligraphy of the name of the temple on it, then Haet'algyŏ which tells us to divest ourselves of agony and restraint, then Ch'ŏnwangmun where Chigukch'ŏnwang, Chŭngjangch'ŏnwang, Kwangmokch'ŏnwang, and Damunch'ŏnwang, all in a word Sach'ŏnwang, which protects Buddhism, are located, and finally we should pass Panyagyo, the bridge of wisdom. Then we find ourselves in the precinct where we can see stone altar and stone bridge starting from the stone embankment. The upper part of the temple implies Buddhist paradise and the lower part represents secular world and the temple can be divided into three areas: Daeungjŏn the main shrine where the statue of Shakamuni is enshrined; Kŭngnakchŏn, the hall of paradise where Amitabha Buddha which has control over Buddhist paradise is enshrined; and Pirojŏn where Pirojanabul which lights Yŏnwhajang world is enshrined.

To reach the upper part of the temple, the part representing Buddhist temple, it was compulsory to pass thirty-three stairs symbolically shaping Torich'ŏn because of the blocking stone altar. Recently, however, for the tourist's sake and for the protection of the stone bridge, it is impossible to pass the stone bridge and a door has been setup in the east-west corridor instead.

Though partly damaged through long years, the stone embankment was made not in artificial way but in natural way of simply building up large and small stones. Such beauty of these stones, large and small, seems to show the difference of magnitude and narrowress of the people.

The stone bridge suspending on the stone altar consists of two pairs of bridges: Ch'ŏngun and Paekun, and Ch'ilbo and Yŏnhwa, and except for a small part the bridge has its original image of its first construction 1200 years before.

This bridge connecting secular world where all creatures live to the Buddhist paradise has rainbow-like gate in the lower part, hence it can be called rainbow bridge, metaphorically bridge of hope and that of bliss.So the bridge consecrates the precinct of the temple, the country of Buddhist.

Rising on the right bridge comprising Ch'ŏngun and Paekun bridges, we can reach Chahamun, a gate surrounded by auspicious signs emanated from Buddha, and Tabot'ap and Sŏggat'ap are seen left and right respectively and between them is seen the main hall of Shakamuni based on Pŏbhwagyŏng, so we can feel we are close to Buddhist paradise.

Tabot'ap and Sŏggat'ap before the main hall, the two pagodas which are called the acme of Shilla's art, were built in the tenth year of the King Kyŏngdŏgk (756) by the prime minister Kim, Dae-Sŏng. But they were not completed before his death and after that the government completed it.

National Treasure No. 20, Tabot'ap is a four-storey pagoda with delicate and beautiful structure on a square cornerstone.

On each edge of the cornerstone is said to have been stone lion at the time of the first construction, but now only one is left.

Opposite to it is Sŏggat'ap, which is also called Muyŏngt'ap meaning a pagoda without shadow. Its structure is simple and magnificant so it is contrasted with skillfully structured Tabot'ap and at the same time they are harmonious enough to add beauty and elegance to Pulguksa.

This three-storey granite pagoda on two-storey cornerstone has a legend of beautifying religious belief and secular love.

During reconstruction and repair work in 1966, at the center of the body of a second storey were found 50cm relic hole, gilded relic case in it, tens of antiquities, and the world's first wooden printed matter, Mugujŏngkwang-daedaranigyŏng and it was named the 126th National Treasure and is displayed at Kyŏngju National Museum.

Besides, many royal palaces and remains are scattered over Pulguksa which has been the very monastery of many monks who protected this country day and night, so Pulguksa, as our precious cultural remains should be protected for ever, not just as sightseeing resort.

The extant Main Hall is what was reconstructed in 1765 (41st year of King Yŏngjo) on the original building through thorough investigation. It is located on the stone embankment big and long with servants' quarters on both sides and it is five kan, unit of length, long and four kan wide.

Inside is Sumidan on central front and on Sumidan is seated Sŏkkasamjonbul, say, with the statue of Shakamuni centered, Buddha-to-be Mirŭgbosal on the left, and Yŏndeŭngbul of the past Kallabosal on the right. So the three statues represent the Buddhas of the past, the present, and the future.

In addition, the statues of two disciples Kasŏb and Anan are seated on the left and right respectively. So, totally five statues are enshrined.

Behind the Main Hall lies Musŏljŏn on stone embankment of seven kan wide. It is said to have been used as lectern by Ŭisangdaesa and his disciples Ojin, P'yohun, and other great monks.

This building shared the same destiny with other buildings of the Pulguksa of being burnt off during Imjinwaeran, of being restored, and of being reconstructed in 1972 to take on the present appearance. The name Musŏl (no lecture) rendered to the lecture hall seems to have too much meaning to be ignored.

The name paradoxically indicates that the transmission of truth and arrival to it can be done through the mediation of language but much bigger meaning will be sprouted from the inside realization.

The Main Hall is surrounded by Tongjangrang in the east, Sŏjangrang in the west, and Namhaengrang in the south, and these three galleries are connected to the Main Hall with Tongigmu and Sŏigmu.

Following Tongjangrang takes us to Unp'an which controls flying creatures and wandering souls in the air, and Mogŏ which is said to rule marine creatures. Following Sŏjangrang to the intersection with Namhaengrang we reach Pŏmyŏngru, called once Sumipŏmjonggak.

As the old name of Sumipŏmjonggak shows it refers to Sumisan (the mountain at the center of the world according to the Buddhist view of the world) and in it, 108 people can be seated and the number of 108 represents symbolically the number of the agonies of man.

One kan wide and two kan long, this small building is, for its stone platform, very famous. The structure of stone platform is unprecedented in world history of architecture: large bottom stone becomes narrower in the middle and upper part again becomes as large as bottom stone and eight columns are made of different kinds of stones and each root goes in gear with others to wear the weathering of long years.

At present, in this building lies Pŏbgo (Buddhist drum) which is said to spread Buddhism for all creatures to repel agony and to achieve emancipation.

On the road leading to Pŏmyŏngru and Sŏigmu behind Sŏjangrang, the gallery in the west to the Main Hall, lie three rows of sixteen stairs.

The number of the stairs is 48 which symbolizes as many wishes of Amitabha.

Stepping down these stairs leads to Kŭngnakchŏn, the Buddhist paradise where Amitabha is seated. We can reach here through Anyangmun, a gate which transforms Buddhist paradise, and through Yŏnhwa Ch'ilbogyo — National Treasure No. 22 — on the left of Ch'ŏngun Paegun-

▼ Snowscape of Pulguksa Temple.

▼ Bleak image of Pulguksa Temple before restoration.

▶ The two stone bridges before restoration Ch'ŏngun-Paegun and Ch'ilbo-Yŏnhwa are the road of monks leading Buddhist world, too.

▼ Precinct of Pulguksa Temple looking hoary.

gyo leading to the Main Hall.

The wooden Kŭngnakchŏn on a firm stone embankment is thought to have been built at the time of the construction of Pulguksa and it was burnt up during Imjinwaeran in 1593 by Japanese invaders. Its reconstruction took place in the 26th year of King Yŏngjo (1750) and it was repaired in 1925. It has in it a sedentary gilded statue of Buddha (National Treasure No. 27), which is 1.66m high and the distance between knees is 1.25m. It wears round face with generous and magnificent feeling.

Near it, surrounding gallery is seen and there was a lecture hall called Kwanghakchanggangshil behind Kŭngnakchŏn.

Behind Kŭngnakchŏn on the right and behind the Main Hall on the left lies Pirojŏn based on Hwaŏmgyŏng (Avatamska Sutra).

It is said to have been 18 kan wide when it was built and to have been burnt up during Imjinwaeran in 1593. After that, it was rebuilt in the first year of Hyŏnjong (1660), but at the end of Yi dynasty this building perished with the site only remained. It was rebuilt in 1973 when Pulguksa was rebuilt.

In this building is seated Pirojanabul (National Treasure No. 26) 1.8m high and 1.36m wide between knees. This statue has the form of left hand taking the index finger of right hand. They say that right hand symbolizes Buddhist world, left one secular world.

On the right corner of the front yard in front of Pirojŏn lies an ownerless stone pagoda for protecting Buddha's relics. It is 2.1m high and takes on a peculiar structure unlike other stupas.

This stone lamp-like stupa has hexagonal ground stone with lotus image engraved and on the stone lies a middle column with a cloud pattern engraved. On this column lies a stone prop to support the body of stupa, the body which has statues of Buddha standing and sedentary in a small space. On the top lie twelve lids of the stupa.

Climbing up the sharp stairs on the right to Pirojŏn, we reach Kwanŭmjŏn in which the Buddhist Goddess of Mercy which can cure disease, avoid difficulties, and deliver blessing if it is invoked is seated.

This Kwanŭmjŏn is located on the highest place of many buildings of Pulguksa and the gate to it is the road to sharp stairs of Musŏljŏn behind the Main Hall.

Built at the time of construction of Pulguksa and reconstructed in the first year of Sŏngjong (1470), Kwanŭmjŏn was burnt up during Imjinwaeran in 1593. Since then, in the 37th year of Sŏnjong (1604), the monk Haech'ŏng rebuilt it and was reworked in 1695 and in 1718 respectively.

At first, there was a statue of Buddhist Goddess of Mercy made of aromatic tree in the 6th year of Shilla's King Kyŏngmyŏng (922), but it perished and what is seated is a standing statue re-made at the time of great reconstruction of Pulguksa in 1973.

① ②

③

① ②Statues of the Four Devas: Chigukch'ŏnwang, protecting in red body the East; Chŭngchang Ch'ŏnwang, living in the 4th layer of Mt. Sumi and protecting the South; Kwangmok Ch'ŏnwang living in the west ridge of Mt. Sumi as outside general of Shakyamuni, and protecting the heaven in the west; and Tamunch'ŏnwang in angry face, protecting the heaven in the north.

③ Ch'ŏngungyo Bridge · Paegungyo Bridge (National Treausre No. 23)

Of the two stairs up and down, the lower 18 stairs are Ch'ŏngungyo Bridge 3.82m high and 5.14m wide. On the center of it is installed a boundary stone and both edges of the arch are touched with the same style of Tabot'ap and Sokkat'ap. Built in the same method of Ch'ŏngungyo Bridge, upper Paegungyo Bridge consists of 16 stairs and it is 3.15m high and 5.14m wide. Passing these bridges and Chahamun, we can reach the front yard Tabot'ap and Sŏkkat'ap are seen in.

▲ Rainbow overpass under Ch'ŏngungyo and Paegungyo Bridges

▶ Ch'ilbogyo Bridge Yŏnhwagyo Bridge — National Treasure No. 22

The lower 10 stairs are Yŏnhwagyo Bridge 2.31m high and 1.48m wide and stairlike boundary stone is installed to divide it and lotus leaves are carved on the stair. On the upper edge of the bridge, arch stone bridge lies. Passing this bridge leads to Ch'ilbogyo Bridge consisting of 8 stairs. This bridge is 4.06m high and 1.16m wide and at the center lies a long stone to divide the left and the right. Passing through Yŏnhwagyo Bridge and Ch'ilbogyo Bridge, we can reach Anyangmun Gate leading to Kŭngnagchŏn.

①

② ③

① **Daeungchŏn (Main Hall), Buddhist seminary of believers, seen between Tabot'ap and Sŏkkat'ap.**

This building 18.6m long and 16.8m wide was reconstructed in 1765 and Sumidan (Sumi Altar) is installed at the front center, on which wooden statues of Shakyamuni, Mirŭgbosal, and Kallabosal are enshrined. On both sides of these statues are standing earthen Kasŏb and Aran, two disciples of Shakyamuni.

② A group of wooden statues consisting of Shakyamuni at the center. Mirŭgbosal, Buddha of future on the left, and Kallabosal, Buddha of the past, on the right.

③ Beautiful gargoyle-like painting of dragon head.

① Tabot'ap — National Treasure No. 20

Built in the 10th year (751) of the 35th king of Shilla, Kyŏngdŏkwang, this pagoda attests that Taboyŏrae praised the teaching of Shakyamuni. (Height 10.4m)

Its base had some stairs in all directions with railings, but now only stone column remains. Upper stair is connected to Kapsŏg, on which five columns are built on each edge and center, and double supports lie to support Kapsŏg. On the Kapsŏg, octagonal pagoda body is laid. On the body lies octagonal stone column like bamboo node to support lotus leaf support. On the lotus leaf support, octagonal lotus pedestal lies to support upper part. The container box for the bones of Buddha is said to have been stolen by Japanese in Japanese colonial rule period. It is said that there were 4 stone lions at the 1st floor of the pagoda body, but now only 1 remains, another is in the British Museum in London, and the whereabouts of the other two is not identified.

①

②

② Sŏkkat'ap — National Treasure No. 21

Frequently called Muyŏngt'ap (pagoda not casting shadow), this stone pagoda symbolizes eternal Buddhism preaching and is representative and the best of Shilla pagodas. Totally, it consists of three stories on two-storied pedestal, which stands on the support consisting of several long stones. The façade stone under has columns at both edges, between which two columns are carved. The body and pedestal are made of one stone respectively. The latter has five-storied support two stories of which are in upper part to support upper body of pagoda and the top of the pagoda that is three-storied pedestal is penetrated by a column and arranged like pierced jades. Around this stone pagoda is a square boundary box, on the four corners and at the center of the four lines of which are installed 8 round lotus pedestal.

④
①
② ③

① Musŏljŏn, an auditorium for the teaching of Buddhism scriptures.
② Mogŏ (wooden fish), said to lead creatures underwater.
③ Buddhist drum located in Pŏmyŏngru.
④ Corridor connecting several buildings of Pulguksa.

Tabot'ap and Sŏkkat'ap

Asadal, a mason of Shilla who completed Tabot'ap was absorbed in making Sŏkkat'ap, but his wife Asanyŏ missed him very much and visited Pulguksa temple, the job site of his husband, from Paekche.

But, the head monk of the temple forbade her to meet her husband for fear that his work would be delayed and only told her to wait until the pagoda is completed.

Asanyŏ who could not meet her husband though she was near him was just told that the shadow of the pagoda would be seen on the Yŏngji lake if the pagoda is completed, so she had only to see the lake impatiently.

One day, white Tabot'ap was reflected on the lake under the light of bright moon.

"Asadal" saying this, she jumped into the lake to embrace the pagoda into which the soul of her husband penetrated.

It was that she saw an illusion in an unbearable yearning.

Asadal, finally completing the pagoda, was told that his wife had been waiting for him, ran to the lake, only to see her cold body.

He, shouting her name, jumped into the water, too. "I forget you for my absorption to art. Neither art nor life is necessary. I will never leave you" leaving this last ejaculation, he shared death with her wife. Both pagodas keeping a heartbreaking legend of the couple, are called Yugŏngt'ap which casts shadow (Tabot'ap) and Muyŏngt'ap which does not (Sokkat'ap).

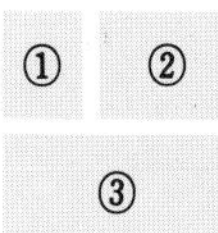

① Wooden Kŭngnakchŏn enshrining Amitabha.

② Kŭmdongamit'a-yŏraechoasung (Gilt bronze sedentary statue of Amitabha) — National Treasure No. 27.

This statue is thought of as taking on original artistry of Korea's own making, getting out of Chinese tradition. It is 166cm high and 125cm wide between knees with merciful face. This masterpiece made of gilt copper is the representative of 9th century unlike the statue in Sŏkkuram.

③Kŭmdong - Pirochanabul - Choasang (Gilt bronze Sedentary Statue of Pirochanabul) National Treasure No. 26.

Built in the same period as the Kŭmdongamit'a - Yŏraechoasang and sharing the characteristics of mode with it, this statue is 177cm high and 136cm wide between the knees. It is brimming with magnificence and generosity and the index finger of right hand indicates Buddhist world and the left hand symbolizing the secular world holds the index finger.

▲ Stupa - Kwanghakpudo - Treasure No. 61

In the form of stone lamp, this stupa is made of red granite. The base stone is engraved with lotus leaf, on which main column stands. The middle pedestal is raised on it and three niches have standing and sedentary statues of Buddha, which composes the round body of the stupa and dodecagonal lid lies on that. This stupa was once taken out to a yard of a restaurant in Tokyo, Japan and taken back to the present place.

▲ Snowscape of the precinct of Pulguksa Temple.

▲ Kwanŭmbosalsang (Statue of the Buddhist Goddess of Mercy)

Located in Kwanŭmchŏn, this statue was made by an artisan ordered by Kyŏngmyŏng then Queen. Its material is Chinese juniper and was respected for its miraculous virtue along with Kwanŭm of Chungsaengsa Temple. It was damaged and the present statue is what was re-made at the time of Pulguksa Temple reconstruction in 1973.

Sŏgguram Bearing the Light of Truth

— National Treasure No. 24 —

Situated on the ridge of the mountain T'oham which was the object of awe of Shilla people for its closer location to the capital than other great mountains of Shilla (Kyeryongsan, Chirisan, T'aebaeksan, P'algongsan), Sŏkkuram was constructed at the 10th year of King Kyŏngdŏk (751) under the name of Sŏgbulsa by the prime minister Kim Dae-sŏng as a part of the building of Pulguksa.

According to Samgukyusa by Ilyŏn (monk in Koryŏ dynasty), Kim Dae-sŏng was born to a poor family and thanks to his offering of farm to a temple he was reincarnated as a son of a highbrow Kim Mun-ryang. Growing up, and hunting bear in the mountain T'oham, he was impressed by something invisible and unknown and he raised Pulguksa for his parents of this world and Sŏgbulsa for his parents of the other world. But it is impossible to know how the original form of Sŏkkuram was, because there is no precise record left.

Judging from the diary Udam Chŏng Shiham wrote during his stay at Sŏkkuram in 1688, "Sŏkkuram is an artificial architecture. Several statues of Buddha are engraved on the rocks on both sides outside stone gate and their ingenuity is beyond description. Stone gates are carved into a rainbow and in the gate lies a great stone statue like a thing alive.

The stone prop is uniformity and ingenuity itself. The lid stone and other stones on the cave are round and standing to be well-balanced. The statues of Buddha standing along look alive and their grotesque images don't allow me to guess their names. Such spectacle is very rare", Sŏkkuram was preserved well until then.

But as national power declines and dark clouds of ruin are hanging over, the incense burner is put off and dilapidated, and this

dilapidation persisted as Japanese colonial rule began.

It is in the colonial rule period that the beautiful marble pagoda which is said to have been located behind the principal statue of Buddha and two Buddhist images in the space were lost and Japanese repaired Sŏkkuram three times.

Through Japanese lavished much money for the care of Sŏkkuram for its beauty, their lack of background of profound principle of Sŏkkuram construction resulted in much damage to Sŏkkuram.

The year 1961 saw deep concern in the preservation of Sŏkkuram with the active support of government and through dehydration in the cave, thermal control, cleansing statue, re-examination of cave structure etc., Sŏkkuram came to take on what it is today.

To get to Sŏkkuram after climbing the ridge of To'ohamsan, it is necessary to pass Sorogil 5-10 minutes through Iljumum which bears a hanging board with the calligraphy of "T'ohamsan Sŏkkuram".

The first to be seen in the precinct of Sŏkkuram is Kamrosu located under the temple in cave. Kamrosu, a mineral water fountain, keeps the legend of Sŏkt'alhae, the 4th king of Shilla, the legend of his hunting before he came to the throne.

This fountain now quenches the thirst of worshippers and tourists and it fills to the brim a big pail as if it cleansed secular restraint and every crime of man.

Now, stepping up the stairs of raw stone on the left, you will get to the entrance to the stone cave temple where the principal image of Buddha is seated.

Entering the temple, tourists can see the statue through transparent glass which is installed to forbid tourists to enter and to protect our precious cultural heritage.

The structure of stone cave temple consists of square frontroom, round backroom, and passage connecting these rooms. In the frontroom are eight carved statues on both sides of wall.

The eight statues have other names like P'albushinjung or Ch'ŏryongp'albu which protects Buddhism in the form of sculpture of congregate gods.

These statues wear armor instead of sacerdotal robe and represent some animal to show their deity.

The first statue on the right of the entrance is a mythical bird called Karura with

▼ Observatory located on the ridge of T'ohamsan.

the nickname of Kŭmshijo whose duty is to protect Buddhism with the strong and lustrous wing.

The second is Kŏndalp'a with a sword to protect Buddhism in the right hand and a bottle of sana, life-giving water in the left hand. The third is a heavenly image, a transformation of great heaven. The fourth is assumed to be a dragon god with a dragon on the head and a magic stone that bestows omnipotence on whoever acquires it in hand. But it is controversial as to the correct names of these statues.

On both sides of the entrance from frontroom to backroom (mainroom) where principal image of Buddha is seated are located two Deva kings with face and bodily muscles showing endless strength and intrepid image.

Bearing another name of Inwangyŏksa, this statue is a chief of gatekeepers for Buddhist state. Its arms stretch upward and downward respectively without any weapon in a stable pose. Its body is full of vividness and emanates invulnerable awe, but without any mischief in the face. The left Deva king stands agape and looks like voicing the sound of [a] so it is called "[a] Deva king". The right one, for the same reason, "[hum] Deva king", which is not easily believable.

Passing both Deva kings and entering a passage called Pido under the arch, you see four heavenly guardians of Buddhism carved on both sides.

The first statue on the right, Dongbang-jigukch'ŏnwang, turns its face eastward with its right hand drawing out a sword, left one stroking the blade in front of its chest, and treading the shoulder of a demon.

Next statue, Pukbang-damunch'ŏnwang, turns its face northward with the right hand raising a pagoda, left hand taking a garment string, and its leg treading the shoulder of a demon.

The first statue on the left, Nambang-ch'ŭngjangch'ŏnwang, treads the back of prostrate demon and takes hold of a sword. Beside it, Sŏbang-kwangmokch'ŏnwang, on the back of a demon takes a sword with left hand and raises right hand to its chest with two fingers bending and the rest stretching, and the fingers seem to mean something, which is difficult to perceive. Its head is not its own, but another face sculptured.

These heavenly guardians, staying in celestial world, supervise people into right life.

Reaching the end of Pido passage and back room, there appears a pair of octagonal columns with lotus pattern adormed on the middle and down parts. One step further inside, it is the very backroom, the main hall of Sŏkkuram, with round pedestal and the statue of Buddha on it, and 15 small statues carved around the main statue.

Total structure of the stone cave consists of 15 saints and disciples of Buddhism carved on the wall of the pedestal, on which statue of Buddha is seated. Except for the front and backside of the statue, there are ten niches. The ceiling of assembled granite looks like the vaulf of heaven, on the center of which lid stone of heaven with lotus engraved is stuck. This lid stone is said to have split into three pieces at the time of construction. So the builder, Kim Dae-sŏng prayed, burning incense, on the mountain then the heaven god descended to attach the split pieces so the construction ended without mishap, which is recorded in Samgukyusa, a historical book.

When it comes to the engraved statues in stone cave, around eleven-faced Buddhist Goddess of Mercy just behind the main statue are engraved 14 standing statues, seven each on both sides.

Around the column near the entrance are Chesŏkch'ŏn (heavenly king of Torich'ŏn next to Four Devas) and Daebŏnch'ŏn (heavenly king controlling secular world located in the first level of Saekkye outside secular world), Behind the column lie wise Munsubosal on the left, which spread Buddhism, and Pohyŏnbosal on the right, which controls Buddha's four virtues.

Behind those, fire statues carved in relief each on both side are those of ten disciples of Shakamuni. These statues are standing ones on circular pedestal and bear circular halo around head.

They are commonly thin and wear surplice but their facial expressions and the things they take in hand are different.

It is impossible to know which statue matches which disciple, but judging from the arrangement and structure of Sŏkkuram, it is likely that they are arranged intersectionally. So, the first statue on the left matches Saribul, a disciple of Shakamuni, and the first on the right Mahamokkŏnnyŏn, who commanded supernatural power and influenced dragon king. In this order, second left matches Mahagansŏp who led disciples after Shakamuni was dead, and second right Subori, the first disciple of Haegong. Third left Puruna, the best disciple in Buddhist sermon and third right, Mahagajŏuyŏu, second to none in the argument about Buddhist law. Fourth left Anayul, excellent in judgment thanks to heavenly eye, fourth right Up'ari, the first disciple in keeping Buddhist law. Fifth left, Lahura, the best disciple in going secetly, fifth right, Anant'a best in listening to others.

The eleven-faced Buddhist Goddess of Mercy on the wall behind the main statue is said to contain truth and the procedure of attaining Buddhahood and it seems to emanate warmth through heavenly habiliment and in its artistic value it is the very masterpiece of masterpieces.

On the upper part of the inner wall are ten niches where Buddha-to-be stayes and Yumagŏsa statues are seated except for the first niches on both sides, which is because Japanese carried two statues out at the end of Yi dynasty.

The main statue of Sŏkkuram is seated on lotus-patterned pedestal of 1.6m high, 3.63m of lower diameter and 2.72m of upper diameter, the pedestal located rather behind the center of the room. The face of the main statue has half-opened eyes which seem to lead people, benevolent mouth as if to preach Buddhism. Every part of the statue has vitality dignity and inaccessibility though it looks generous and soft.

▼ Sunrise seen from T'ohamsan, the first landing place of the sun rising from the East Sea.

Besides, most Buddha statues have halo just behind head but on the contrary the halo of the statues is separated a little and has lotus pattern. It is located on the upper wall of eleven-faced Buddhist saint so any worshipper can see the halo behind its face and according to the watching position, that of halo also moves to bear cubic effect.

The figure of its hands is Ch'okchihangmain which means the moment of demonstrating Buddha's realization of the Buddha repeled the temptation of devil and touched soil.

Mixed with religious meaning, artistic value, and high level of scientism, the structure of Sŏkkuram is intended to enjoy the first ray of rising sun from the East Sea. The ray reflected on the face of the main statue again this time lights all sides including several sculptures. So it is as if the light of truth made clear all creatures.

The following photographs are miniatures of Sŏkkuram displayed at Tongak Art Museum in Folk Craft Village, Kyŏngju. For many tourists and worshippers to understand the mystery of Sŏkkuram, the very representative of Shilla's art, this photograph is included here at the courtesy of the Art Museum. (Tongak Art Museum is run by an individual, without any support of government. It is the place for the study of Shilla's science history and receives donation from views, but not admission fee.)

22

Kamnosu, curing a subordinate of a bad habit

Before Sŏg, T'al-hae, the 4th king of Shilla, came to the throne, he enjoyed hunting on T'ohamsan mountain.

One day, he was hunting on the mountain and ordered a subordinate to fetch water to quench his thirst.

The subordinate wanderĕd about to find water and finally found a well under a rock overlooking East Sea. He filled small gourd vessel with water and returned. Being thirsty, he tried to drink the water a little, but his mouth stuck fast to the vessel.

Thinking long with pains, he decided to ask the king-to-be T'alhae pardon and went to see him with his mouth adhered to the vessel, and said, "I will never try to drink water before you do from now on anywhere." At that, vessel fell apart. People call this well Yonaejŏng since.

Miniature 1, the front of Sŏkkuram.

Miniature 2, helping viewers understand the round main hall of Sŏkkuram, by dividing anteroom, pido, and vault.

Miniature 3, showing eleven-faed Buddhist Goddess of Mercy behind the principal image of Buddha, by dividing it and Vault.

Miniature 4, the front of Sŏkkuram.

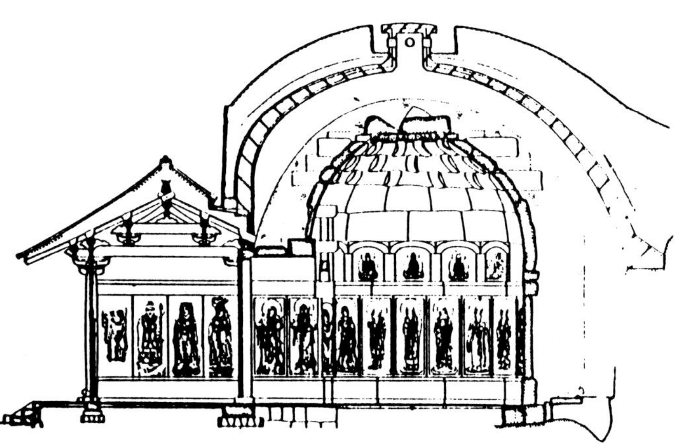
Cross section of southern Sŏkkuram.

Cross section of northern Sŏkkuram.

Sedentary statue of Shakyamuni, the principal image of Buddha of Sŏkkuram, on a stone lotus pedestal.

From the benevolent face to teach people and all parts of the body, life force emits. It also has dignity not allowing easy access, so it evokes mystery.

Namsan, Holy Place of Shilla Culture

Located four kilometers away from downtown Kyŏngju, in an oval form, Namsan is 4km long from east to west and 8km from south to north; its altitude is 468m. Though every mountain in this area is full of heritage and legends, Namsan is the very center of Shilla culture to the extent that the history of Shilla stemmed and closed here.

One thousand year have passed since Shilla perished and in spite of that, every valley and corner of Namsan cherishes Buddha statue and stone pagoda. Every rock, large and small, is permeated with a legend, so any tourist could breathe the aroma of Shilla.

Namsan, at once a pure land and paradise for Shilla people, though not large nor magnificant, is in itself a panorama with its ever-changing valley and curious rocks. The mountain is our precious cultural heritage.

Namsan roughly consists of 35 valleys, which are divided into three sections: Tongnamsan from Wanggjŏnggol closest to Panwolsŏng, Shilla's old palatial site, to the 16th Pongwhagol southward; Namnamsan including Yangjoamgol, Shimsogol, Paegungol, and Ch'ŏnwangjisan with the last centered; and Sŏnamsan from Ch'ŏnryonggol to Shikhyegol. Tongnamsan with a big valley of 1.5km long has 29 temple sites, 39 statues, 27 stone pagodas, and about 10 stone lamps.

In Namnamsan were found 6 temple sites, 2 statues, 2 stone pagodas and 4 stone lamps. Sŏnamsan has a big valley of 2.5km long with a gentl slope, on which 71 temple sites, 37 statues, 34 stone pagodas, and 9 stone lamps were found. So Namsan in Kyŏngju can be called an unprecedented open museum in the world.

① Group of Stone Statues on an Cliff of Ch'ilbulam rock of Mt. Namsan. - Treasure No. 200.

For the three embossed statues of Buddha on the rock and the four embossed ones on a stone column, the name Ch'ilbulam (meaning seven stone statues) was made. The three statues are relieved on a rock of 426cm high and the height of them is 260cm. Two attending statues are 210cm high and the four statues on columns are 223-242cm high, different according to the height of the column. They have swollen eyes and large nose, smiling still. Its poise is imposing for strength and benevolence (Unified Shilla Dynasty)

② Namsan - Yongchangsagog - Sŏgbulchoasang (Sedentary stone statue of Buddha at Yongchangsa Temple Val|ley in Mt. Namsan) - Treasure No. 187.

Three-storied pedestal made of processed even rock and 3 drum-like columns supports sedentary image of Buddha (sitting with legs crossed). Its head disappeared and the other parts are preserved comparatively well.

The statue, 4.56m high, sculptured in the period of Unified Shilla is similar to that in the niche of Sŏkkuram with its refinement and tension.

③ Yongchangsagog - Samch'ŭngsŏkt'ap (Three-storied stone pagoda at Yongchangsa Temple Valley - Treasure No. 186.

Standing on the highest peak of east range surrounding Yongchangsa Temple site in the valley of that name, this pagoda, on a big rock as its pedestal, has its upper base and three-storied body on the base. Though small with the height of 4.2m, it seems to be connected to heaven for its location on the peak.

P'osokchŏngchi - Historic Site No. 1

Playground of Shilla kings or the site of the palace of the queen, this was called the site of Sŏng-nam detached palace. The royal palace that seems to have been has perished and what is left is an abalone-like structure thought to be used as an outing place with recitation of poems.

The size is 35cm wide, 26cm long and total length is 10m with brilliant Namsan as its setting.

Legend has it that when the 49th king of Shilla, Hŏngang was playing near P'osŏkchŏng, a god of Mt. Namsan appeared to dance and the king followed suit, from which a dance named Ŏmusamg-shimmu was made. Also, it is said that Kyŏngaewang in 927 was playing here when the king of Post-Paekche, Kyŏnhwon invaded, so the former had to committed suicide, so the millennium of Shilla ended here.

28

Namsan and Mangsan, former body of gods

Sŏrabŏl, the first land to be shone at the beginning of the world. To this land umber-faced and masculine mangod and round-faced woman-goddess with shining eyes were coming.

"Bravo! This is the very place we will live in." They exclaimed. Then, a virgin washing at the riverbank, surprised at their cry, looked at the two enormous gods move toward her "Look the mountains" saying this, she feigned. Hearing the cry of the girl, the gods stopped, then they could not move again. They changed into mountains on the spot for her cry.

So, both gods came to embrace Kyŏngju and, as the girl said, became mountains, to share the same destiny with it.

Man-god, collecting dark rock and brown soil, became the magnificent Namsam, and the goddess, Mangsan risen soft and comfortable to the west of Namsam.

Namsant'apkog - Maaechosanggun (Group of statues on a cliff at T'apkog in Mt. Namsan) Treasure 201.

On a rock about 9m high and some 26m round in girth, tens of statues of Buddha are sculptured pictorially, so this rock is also called Rock of Buddha. Southern sculptures of this rock (upper picture), of Buddha and Buddha-to-be sit on a big lotus and on a flower respectively. The latter clasps its own hands in prayers with its head turned toward the former. The former inclines itself toward the latter, to arouse kind and free mood. The line of both, however, is hard to see for defacement. Eastern sculptures (lower picture) of principal Buddha on a big lake and of small attending Buddha-to-be on a small lotus have the same pose and destiny as southern ones. On the head of the Buddha, six flying images are engraved and a monk upholding a censer is carved.

Namsanmirŭggog - Sŏgbulchoasang (Sedentary Stone Statue at Mirŭg Valley of Mt. Namsan) Treasure No. 136

Enshrined in Borisa Temple where nuns practice asceticism, 250m distant from Mirŭg Valley of Mt. Namsan, this statue is called Borisachi-Sŏgbulchoasang (Sedentary Stone Statue at Borisa Temple Site). The statue is 2.44m high and its pedestal is 1.92m. It has big pedestal and halo, so it is a perfect statue though it has some crack and is preserved comparatively well.

Made of white granite in Unified Shilla Dynasty, it has generous internal smile.

Legend of Vagina Valley

It was in the reign of the Queen Sŏndŏk.

One day in the midst of winter, many frogs had been croaking for several days in Ongmunchi lake of Yŏngmyosa temple.

"Croaking of frogs in wintertime". It is a mysterious occasion so the people reported it to the queen.

Being told, the queen, after long thought, called in two generals Al-ch'ŏn and P'il-t'an to select two thousand crack troops and to go defeat the hidden enemy troops in Vagina Valley.

The generals, leading one thousand picked soldiers respectively, went westward. They asked for the location of the Vagina Valley and encircled it. Then they made a surprise attack on five hundred Paekche troops hiding in the vally. The enemy troops were annihilated.

Also, Paekche's flying column hiding behind the rocks of Namsanryŏng and the rear guard of 1300 soldiers were defeated after a fierce battle.

Being struck with admiration for the queen's clairvoyance of seeing through the raid of enemy troops, the courtiers asked how he had known it.

"The face of angry frog is the same as that of a soldier, which indicates a disaster in the army. Considering the fact that frogs are croaking in Ongmunchi lake, Ongmun meaning the vulva, woman symbolizing Yin, Yin transferred to white, white indicating the west, I could think enemy troops were hiding in the topography like Ongmun.

And, penis shrinks in vulva, so I thought the enemy hiding in the valley would be defeated easily. Listening to such explanation, all courtiers and servants were surprised.

① ②

① Maaesŏkka - Yŏraedaechoabul (Big Sedentary Statue of Buddha on a Cliff) Kyŏngsangbuk-do Tangible Cultural Properties No. 158.

Engraved on a big rock on the mountain ridge where curious rocks rise behind Sansŏnam of Samnŭng Valley, this statue 5.21m high and 3.5m wide between knees is enshrined on a lotus pedestal. Its head is embossed from a large rock and its body is line-engraved in harmony with nature.

② Sŏch'ulchi (Lake of Book Yielding) Historic Site No. 138

Legend puts it that the 22nd king of Shilla, Sochi, prevented Kungchu and a monk from assassinating himself with the writing "Shoot the case of Korean harp" shown in the book the old man rising from the lake presented.

T'ongilchŏn (Unification Hall)

This hall, located on the ridge of Mt. Dongnam, was completed in 1977. It enshrines the portraits of the Shilla kings, T'aechongmuyŏl, Munmu, and Hongmu (Commander-in-chief, Kim, Yu-shin) who contributed to the unification of Shilla. It is filled with national wish and will to liquidate the past tragedy and to accomplish unification. On both sides and behind the main hall is installed a gallery, in which a documentary picture of unification by Shilla is displayed.

① ② ④ ⑤
⑥
③ ⑦

① Gallery around Main Hall, with documentary picture of unification displayed.
② Sŏwonmun Gate in T'ongilch'ŏn.
③ Picture of Glory of Unification.
④ Main Hall of T'ongilchŏn which portraits of the Shilla king's T'aechongmuyŏl, Munmu and Kim, Yu-shin are enshrined.
⑤ Picture of Bottlefield of the king Mugyŏl at Namch'ŏnchŏng.
⑥ Picture of bloody fight at Hwangsanbŏl field.
⑦ Picture of annihilation of T'aag troops at Maesosŏng Castle.

Hwarang Institution of Learning.

It is a Korean style hall for spiritual discripline, built on the land of 36,000 P'yŏng. The ideology of Hwarangdo, fidelity, faith, trust, courage, generosity based on Confucianism, Buddhism and Taoism, became the motive power of unification of the three kingdoms. To succeed such sublime spirit, this hall was built and main trainees are high school and college students.

① Whole view of Hwarang Institution, magnificent in the architectural beauty of Shilla.
② Entrance view to Hwarang Institution of Learning.
③ Side view of Hwarang Institution of Learning.
④ Hwarang Institution, the hall for spiritual discipline of the adolescece.

Tumuluses Enabling Us to Feel a Single Body with Two Millenniums' Time and Space

Any tourist to Kyŏngju could have a feeling of a single body with two thousand years as well as the weight of history, for a series of tumuluses scattered over the city.

Giving stronger feeling of thousand-year old capital than the brilliant Pulguksa, Sŏkkuram and golden crown, these tumuluses are the vital existence of Kyŏngju.

These tumuluses have dignity in silence and give intimacy of conversation beyond a millennium's time and space.

They cluster in tens or twenties and they are: Central Great Tumuluses located at the center of downtown; Sŏndosan Tumuluses where Muyŏlwang Tomb lies, Kŭmgangsan Tumuluses where T'alhaewang Tomb lies, Sŏnamsan Tumuluses where tombs of Park's family are located; Tongnamsan Tumuluses where Hŏngangwang Tomb lies; Namsan Tumuluses where Sŏndŏkwang Tomb lies.

The 56 tombs of as many Shilla kings may be part of the tumuluses, but only 38 are identified and even so, their identifications are not correct exept for some.

Mankind from early times has intered dead bodies and some facilities for interment are prepared and some ground mark was raised.

During the period of Three Kingdoms, the mound was made of stones and soils in circular type, square type or gourd type.

Shilla's tumuluses are circular earthen ones and large tomb has 82m of ground diameter and 22m of height.

Gourd type tumulus is that of two small tumuluses connected, which is for couple or father and son. Kyŏngju has 10 gourd type tumuluses and the largest is the number 98 tomb (Hwangnamdaebun) which is 83m in diameter and 25m in height located in Tumulus Park.

Square type tumulus is that of square base and there is only one located at the road leading to Pulguksa.

The interal structure of these tumuluses is different according to the period in which they were made and Chŏksŏkmokkwakpun and Sŏkshilbun are representatives.

The former is made by digging up the ground to make a room to bury wooden box, on which stones of the size of man's head are accumulated with clay. After that, tomb is raised.

The latter, considering moisture, is made by both digging up the ground to make a room and laying wooden box. Then the body is laid with every personal outfittings worn on the body and the remaining space in the coffin and the box lain is filled with burial accessories. Such kind of tomb has a lithic square inside and entrance. The size of the inside is 1-3m in height.

Before anything else, a lithic coffin with dead body and burial accessories are put and lithic gate of inside is raised and earthen tomb is made.

The relics found in the tumuluses are personal ornaments of the hero, daily necessities, weaponry, horse equipments and precious tools.

Burying these accessories with the body was religiously meant to enable it to live conveniently in afterlife.

These accessories found show characteristics of Shilla culture, cultural interchange between three kingdoms, internationality of Shilla culture, and aspect of Shilla People's life, so they are very precious cultural heritage.

Tumuluses in Daerŭngwon.

▲ Guide Map of Daerŭngwon.

Located at the edge of Kyŏngju, this tumulus garden of 20 tombs is the largest of all tumuluses in the city.

These tumuluses are located on level ground and their scale is great. To them Kŭmgwanch'ong where five unprecedented golden crowns and precious heritage were found Sŏbongch'ong, Kŭmryŏngch'ong, Ch'ŏnmach'ong, number 98 Ssanggobun belong.

Beside them lies the tomb of Mich'uwang, the 7th generation posterity of Kim, Al-ji, the first Shilla king coming from the Royal family Kim. This tomb is also called Chukchangnŭng, and according to the historical book Samgukyusa the reason is: After the King Michin, in the 14th Yuryewang's reign, Yisŏguk suddenly invaded Shilla unprepared for foreign invasion, so Shilla soldiers had hard times.

At this time, strange soldiers appeared to help Shilla army to defeat the enemy troops. The helpers all wore bamboo leaves and after they beat the enemy they disappeared falling the bamboo leaves. At that, people thought the late king helped, so since then the tumuluses are called Chukchangnŭng or Chukhyŏnnŭng ("Chuk" means bamboo).

Number 155 tumulus, Ch'ŏnmach'ong, has gallery-like inside for the people to see easily. Its ground diameter is 47m and

Burial accessories are laid on a pile of stones inside wooden box and around wooden coffin. Near the head of the body lie golden crown, silver belt, glass beads, and near the leg lies gilt bronze shoes, iron ax. On the left lies such personal weapon as a height is 12.7m, and it shows a typical structure of Chŏksŏkmokkwagbun.

sword with circular handle and on the right iron ax, iron spear, iron arrowhead.

Besides, many burial accessories were found. Especially the picture of flying horse on a plane of 75cm in width 53cm in length and 0.6cm in thickness, a plane made of the barks of birch, describes a horse flying on a cloud to arouse mysticism.

② ③

① Dwarfishness of tourists walking on Sorogil between Tumuluses enlarges the enormity of the tumulus.

② **Mich'uwangnŭng (Tumulus of the King Mich'u)-Historic Site No. 175**

Thirteenth king of Shilla, King Mich'u is said to have been born in Kyerim and he is the 7th generation grandson of Kim, Alchi, the founder of Kim family. He defeated Paekche troops at Pongsan and Koesan castles and encouraged agriculture. His reign spans from A.D. 262-284 (for 23 years).

③ **Hwangnamdaech'ong (Hwangnam Great Tumulus)**

The largest tumulus (height: 25m base diameter: 83m) of Shilla tumulus, this consists of two tumuluses and is called No. 98 tumulus.

④ Whole view of Daerŭngwon.

Manp'ashikchŏk of the king Munmu

Shinmundaewang, the 31st king of Shilla, built Kamŭnsa temple at the location where Daewangam the tomb of the king Munmu is seen, to commemorate his father, Munmudaewang. In May 1st of the next year, a marine official reported that "a small island is flowing and ebbing following the tide toward Kamŭnsa temple".

Thinking it strange, the king ordered the seer to predict what will happen.

"The late king, Munmudaewang, as the guardian deity, became the dragon of East Sea and the late general Kim, Yu-shin, as a sun of 33 heavens, was reincarnated as a courtier. Both saints intend to endow you with a treasure to defend the country, so if you go to the seashore, you will get a precious thing", the seer said.

Being pleased, the king went to Igyŏndae (Historic Site No. 159) on the 7th of the month and ordered messenger to examine

Now, Your Highness, make a bamboo fife of it, and all the country will be peaceful.

Surprised and pleased, the king had the bamboo felled and came out of the sea, and the mountain and the dragon disappeared.

The son (Hyosowang) of the king, congratulating his father on the news said "The notchmark of this jaded belt is a genuine dragon". As the king asked how he knew that, the son took off the second notchmark and dropped it in the stream.

The notchmark changed into a dragon and ascended to heaven and a lake was made on the spot, which was named Yongyŏn (dragon lake). Since then, this fife was preserved in Ch'ŏnchongo. When this fife is played, enemy troops retreat, diseases disappear, drought is appeased, flood clears up, wind goes down, and the sea goes down.

the mountain floating on the water. The geographical feature of the mountain is like the head of a turtle, on which a bamboo is planted. It becomes two at daytime and one at nighttime.

On the next day, when the bamboo becomes one at noon, the world vibrated and it stormed and got dark. Such state continued for a week and on the 16th of the month the wind and the sea went down.

Then, the king went near the mountain by ship and entered the mountain. A dragon appeared and presented him with a jaded belt. Receiving the belt, the king asked "why the bamboo became united and divided."

As both hands are needed to make a sound, so bamboo should be united to produce a sound. All this phenomenon portends that your highness will govern the country with a sound.

So, this fife is called Manp'ashikchŏk (meaning fife which puts down wave) and preserved as a national treasure, which is recorded in Samgukyusa.

Ch'ŏnmach'ong

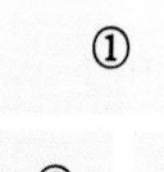

① Whole view of Ch'ŏnmach'ong.
② Ch'ŏnmado Changni (Picture of flying horse drawn on mudguard attached to horse waist.)
Changni is a kind of mudguard suspending on the horseback and it is made of folded barks of birch. Its size is 75cm wide, 53cm long and 0.6cm thick. It is ornamented with 10cm-wide arabesque design of dried honeysuckle on each side and a picture of flying horse is described on the center. Its image is realistic and mysterious.
③ Necklace, thought to be worn by the dead intered.
- Treasure No. 619 (5-6th century length: 63cm)

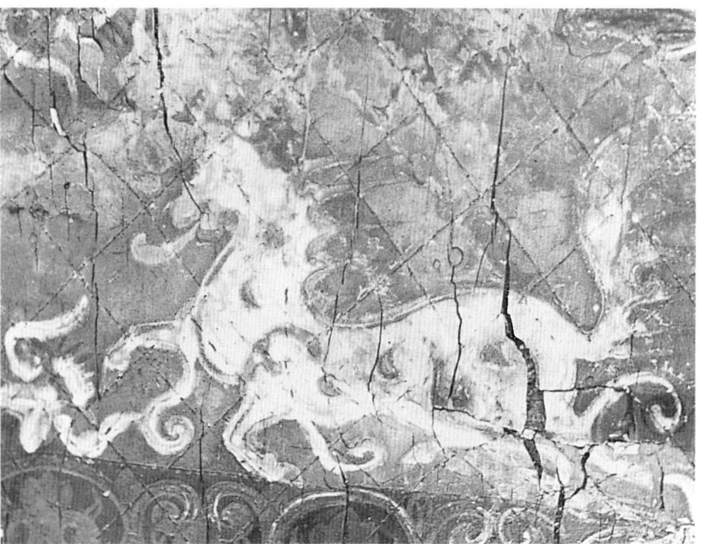

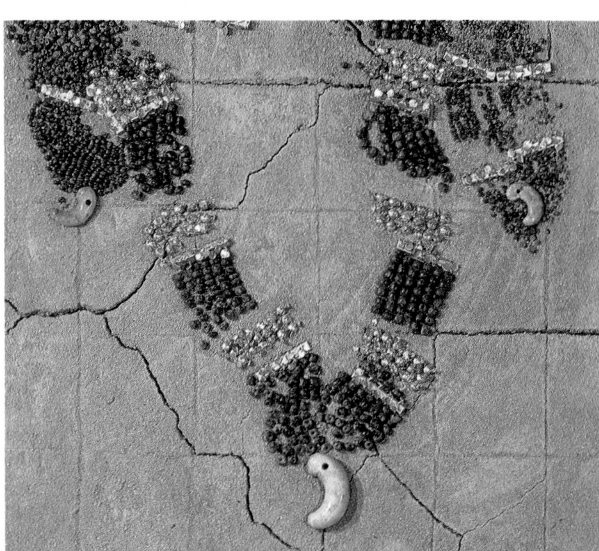

T'aejong-muyŏlwangnŭng (Tomb of the King T'aejong-muyŏl)

① ② ③

① Whole view of the Tumulus of the King T'aechongmuyŏl.
② Turtle-shaped base and Isu of the monument for the Tumulus of the King T'aechongruyŏl. - National Treasure No. 25
③ Tumuluses around Mt. Sŏndo where Tumulus of the King T'aechongmuyŏl is located.

Located under Sŏndosan, this tomb for the 29th King T'aejong-muyŏl is a circular one with 110m of circumference and 11m of height. Large stone is buried under the tomb as a guard stone.

The king in question, T'aejong-muyŏl, is a grandson of the 25th King Chinjiwang and his name is Ch'unch'u. His grandfather, Chinjiwang, was ousted for misgovernment and his posterity barely succeeded to the power with the help of Kim, Yu-shin.

Before he was enthrored, Kim, Ch'unch'u went to Koguryŏ, Japan, T'ang to break international isolation and achieved Shilla-T'ang alliance for the unification of the three kingdoms: Koguryŏ, Paekche, and Shilla. Taking office as a king, he annexed Paekche and died on the way to annexing Koguryŏ.

In the tablet house in front of the tomb lies a tombstone without the main body. But the monument base in the shape of a turtle and upper part ornament remain. For the excellent engraving of the remaining parts of this monument, Tombstone of the king T'aejong-muyŏl (National Treasure No. 25), this tombstone is very famous. The upper part ornament is made of six dragons standing on the fore legs, the dragons holding up the epitaph "T'aejongmuyŏldaewangjimyo". Their hind legs lift a magicstone that bestows omnipotence on whoever acquires it. The turtle on the base seems to march.

Behind this tomb lie 4 anonymous tombs and across the road lie the tombs of Kim, Yang and Kim, In-mun. On the mid-slops of the mountain to the north, behind the Sŏaksŏwon are located the tombs of the 24th king, Chinhŭngwang, the 25th Chinjiwang the 46th Munsŏngwang, and the 47th Hŏnanwang.

Wonsŏngwangnŭng (Historic Site No. 26)

① Whole view of the King Wonsŏng and Koerŭng.
② Stone Lion.

Located a little far from the road leading to Ulsan from Kyŏngju, Wonsŏngwangnŭng is known as Koerŭng (Suspended tomb) to us. Standing on lithic column rail and guard stone of 12 animals — mouse, cow, tiger, rabbit, dragon, snake, horse, sheep, monkey, cock, dog, pig — it has stone plane in front and stone lions statue of literary man, and statue of a general are symmetrically positioned.

Of these stone statues, stone lions and statue of a general are excellent works enough to represent Shilla's fine art. The former open their eyes with a fierce glare and throw out their chest. On their hairy necks is suspended a beaded necklace and the tails are raised to their back.

Of the four lions, the one with smile on the mouth and turned head shows the craftmanship of Shilla people. One of the fore legs raised symbolizes endless action and courage to beat his opponent. This lion, unlike the other three lions standing erect, is permeated with artistic virtuosity showing readiness to attack anytime.

The statue of a general wears hood and has long eyes and high nose, shutting his mouth tight. He also wears heavy beard.

His sleeves turned up and one hand doubles its fist and the other one takes a stinging club. His clothes is a long coat and his waist is turning backward with the whole weight centered on one leg. Its bones and sinews are strong enough to be equal to those of the Deva king of Sŏkkuran.

Statue of Soldier.

Orŭng (Five Tombs)

① Orŭng seen from entrance.
② Inside of Submarine tumulus.

Located to the right of the Kŭmsŏngro Road leading to the downtown from the access road of the highway, Orŭng is the site of Park, Hyŏggŏse, the founding father of Shilla and his wife, Alyŏng, the second king to the fifth without the fourth, Namhaewang, Yuriwang, and P'arawang.

Orŭng is also called Sarŭng (Snake tomb) for the reasŏn that according to Samgugyusa, historical book, the founding father died after 61-year reign and seven days later the remains was scattered on the ground and the queen was also dead. So they tried to hold a funeral for them together, but a snake appared to disturb. Thinking this phenomenon a heavenly will, they held five funerals for the four limbs and torso.

Orŭng is a kind of sacred ground for Shilla people because five founding fathers of Shilla take an everlasting rest.

Daewangam, subaqueous tomb of Munmudaewong

Erected for the wish of Munmuwang that "Though dead, I will defend my country forever as a dragon", this tomb indicates a rock island 250m off the Ihyŏndae where Munmuwang was said to have changed into a dragon. We can reach Ihyŏndae by following the road to Kamp'o after passing Pomun Tourist Complex from Kyŏngju.

Born as the elest son to T'aejongmuyŏlwang, Munmuwang with his father, overthrew Paekche in 1660 (7th year of Muyŏlwang). When his father died conquering Koguryŏ in 661 he returned to accede to the throne. In 668, with T'ang dynasty he conquered P'yŏngyang Castle and Koguryŏ as well. After that, when T'ang tries to rule the ex-territory of Koguryŏ with local government, he expelled T'ang troops and achieved perfect unification of the Korean Perinsula.

21 years after he became king, he died with a message that "though I become a dragon, I have no wish if I can defend my motherland". The son of the late king, Shinmunwang cremated the remains following the intention of the father and buried the ashes in the rock island.

This subaqueous tomb is unprecedented in the world and in a large rock island with the perimeter of 200m is made a cruciform waterway. A lithic box is laid underwater 4 P'yŏng wide and the box is closed with a lid stone. The tomb is always drenched in clean water, because the wave is pushed from the east waterway.

Tomb of T'aedaegaggan Kim, Yu-Shin

— Historic Site No. 21 —

① Bronze statue of the General Kim, Yu-shin.
② Whole view of the tumulus of General Kim, Yu-shin.

Crossing Sŏch'ŏngyo suspended across Sŏchŏn, a tributary of Hyŏngsangang river near Kyŏngju Express Terminal and following Hŭngmuro, we can reach the tomb of Kim, Yu-shin, key member of the unification of three kingdoms.

Kim, Yu-shin, the 12th posterity of Kayan King Kim, Su-ro and the son of Shilla's famous general, Sŏhyŏn, was born in Chinch'ŏn in 595.

He became a Hwarang, Shilla's elite course member to raise generals, at the age of 15 and rendered distinguished services in the battles with Paekche and Koguryŏ. After that he enthroned Kim, Ch'un-ch'u (Muyŏlwang) and conquered the two kingdoms to be a hero in uniting the Korean Peninsula.

Appreciating his achievements, the king graced him with the title of T'aedaegaggan paid tribute to him by gracing him with the title of Hŭngmuwang.

His tumulus has plane guard store under the tomb and the guard stone has statues of 12 animals beautiful enough to match a national hero.

①　②
③　④

① Tumulus of the King T'alhae - Historic Site No. 174

Soil-accumulated round tumulus, this is for the 4th king of Shilla, Sŏk, T'al-hae (height: 7m diameter: 10m)

② Tumulus of the King Sŏngdŏk - Historic Site No. 28

Tumulus of the 33rd king of Shilla, Songdŏk, this is the first tumulus equipped with perfect form in Shilla, including plane stone as guard stone, 12 statues of 12 animals in front of guard stone, two statues of literary man, and as a many statues of soldier. But all of them perished and 4 stone lions are positioned on both sides of the front and back. This tumulus is estimated to have been built in early Unified Shilla period.

③ Tumulus of the King Shinmun - Historic Site No. 181

The 31st king of Shilla, Shinmun (681-692) established national teaching institute and Wihwabu, put all administration in order, and contrived cultural renaissance. This tumulus has brick-like processed stones accumulated in five layers, on which a plane stone is added. (Height: 7m diameter: 10m)

④ Square Tumulus in Kuchŏng-ri - Historic Site No. 27.

Of many Shilla tumuluses, this is a rare example of square tumulus, which has four columns on each edge, column made of three-storied processed stone, and long stone is lifted on it. At the center of southern façade lies entrance. The inside is stone chamber and lithic coffin support lies on the floor. On each outside, three statues of animals are engraved and arranged. (Height: 2m Length of each façade: 9.5m)

National Kyŏngju Museum, Treatury of Cultural Assets

▲ Whole view of National Kyŏngju Museum

Located at Inwang-dong, Kyŏngju, National Kyŏngju Museum originated from Kyŏngju Shilla Association organized to protect cultural assets by the citizen of Kyŏngju in 1910.

This organization was inaugurated formally as Kyŏngju Hotoric Spot Protection Association in 1913 and collected every remains scattered across Kyŏngju to display at an inn in Tongbu-dong, which is the first exhibition.

In 1926, it became Kyŏngju branch of Chosŏn Government-General Museum and by the time of independence of Japan, it was named Kyŏngju Branch of National Museum. Then, by the museum extension plan of the government it moved to the present locus in 1975.

Current National Kyŏngju Museum is a large one with the site of 20,705 P'yŏng, the floor space of 3,107 P'yŏng, and the gallery of 820 P'yŏng.

The gallery consists of two-storied main gallery with Korean traditional roof and Western style building, two single-storied outhouses on both sides of the main building. In sum, 2,500 relics are displayed for the public.

The main building displays the relics of prehistoric times to Unified Shilla Era collected in Kyŏngju in 8 exhibition halls.

Hall one shows relics of neolithic age, bronze age and early iron age in the historical order.

The relics of neolithic age (B.C. 4000-B.C. 1000) comprise rubbed stoneware excavated in Hup'ori, Uljin-gun. Bronze age (B.C. 800-ca A.D. 1) relics are red porcelain excavated across Kyŏngsang-do, unpatterned earthenware, brilliantly patterned earthenware, rubbed stone sword, arrowhead, stone plough, adze, and other earthenwares. Iron age (ca. A.D. 100) relics are bronze ax, bronze spear, small bronze sword, curb, parts of cart, mirror, belt, all of which were found at Kujŏng-dong, Kyŏngju, Ŏŭn-dong, Yŏngch'ŏn, P'yŏngri-dong, Taegu, and Ipsil-ri, Wolsŏng-gun.

Room Two for Shilla earthenware displays various iron weaponry excavated at Choyang-dong, Kyŏngju, bronze mirror, black rubbed earthenware, unpatterned earthenware of Han dynasty, urn, curved urn, brazier-like earthenware, curved dish, and iron point excavated at Hwangsŏng-dong, Kyŏngju, and long-necked urn with horn-like handle, pocket-like earthenware, and iron ax which represent the period of the first Three Kingdoms (A.D. 0-300) and earthenware and clay icon of the second Three Kingdoms.

Room Three and Four are for the relics donated by Kugŭn Lee, Yang-sŏn who during his tenure at College of Medicine, Kyŏngbuk University collected many relics of the period spanning from prehistory to Chosŏn Dynasty.

Classified by materials, these relics are made of stone, earth, mineral, iron, and jade. Periodically it is also very various. Regionally, his donated relics were excavated mainly at Taegu, Kyŏngju where he had many chances to explore, and these relics are invaluable in the study of prehistoric history of the province.

His collection donated here comprises metallic works (323 works of 142 kinds), jaded works (193 works of 43 kinds), earthenware (144 works of 102 kinds), bone and horn (2 works of 2 kinds), others (4 works of 4 kinds). These relics were specially exhibited at the outhouse 1, National Kyŏngju Museum for 3 months from Sep. 15, 1986 – Dec. 15, 1986 followed by another one-

▼ National Kyŏngju Museum, vivified with the architectural beauty, permeated even in a column.

month special exhibition at National Central Museum. Since then, they are exhibited at the present site.

Dedicated to medicine and collection of cultural assets and afraid of their being dispersed, Lee, Yang-sŏn came to donate them for their publicity, and to commemorate his donation, his profile carved on jade is erected at the entrance to the room.

Room 5 for Hwangryongsa temple has a miniature of the temple and a part of forty thousand relics, the temple where one of Shilla's three treasures Changyukchonsang and nine-storied wooden pagoda lay and every king of Shilla went to listen to the lecture of 100 hundred great monks.

Room 6 is for tile, brick and United Shilla's earthenware. The convex tile has patterns of lotus, Posanghwa, honeysuckle, flowering plant, Chinese phoenix, giraffe, and lion. Also the tiles used as the ridge of tiled roof and the bricks with the patterns of lotus, arabesque, and hunting scene are displayed.

The earthenware of Unified Shilla Dynasty comprises round box with low base, long-necked bottle, narrow-mouthed bottle with large base, lidded box, rectangular bottle, and urn for containing ashes.

Room 7 is for Buddhism mechanical art and inscription on stone monument. After bronze culture was introduced to Korea and developed rapidly, metallic art products were made during the period of Three Kingdoms, and in the age of Unified Shilla Dynasty very refined and various works on the basis of Buddhism were made. Especially, tools and bowls for Buddhist ritual show excellent culture in the field of moulding.

Of the relics displayed the followings are of importance: a series of the bowls for Buddha's bones found in Sŏkkat'ap (the pagoda of Shakyamuni) in the precinct of Pulguksa; a bowl for Buddha's bones and golden bowl with tree pattern found in the five-storied brick pagoda in Songnimsa Temple; a bowl for the same purpose found at the three-storied stone pagoda in Kalhangsa Temple site; bronze bell of Koryŏ Dynasty found in Kulbulsa Temple site; bronze weight of twelve animals found in Sŏngdong-dong, Kyŏngju; a written record of pagoda on a gilt bronze found in the Yŏmgŏhwasang stupa (owned by Seoul National Museum), the oldest stupa in Korea.

Room 8 is for sculpture and the things displayed are: gilt bronze Amitabha Samjonsang in the form of Ilgwangsamjonbul of the period of Three Kingdoms; the head of gilt bronze Buddha-to-be excavated in Hwangryongsa Temple site; stone Pangasayusang found in Sŏak-dong, comparable to those in the National Central Museum or to that made of wood in Japan, Stone Samjonbul of Tab-ri; a statue of standing Yaksa Buddha of Paekryulsa Temple, called one of three great gilt bronze images of Buddha with Amitabha of Pulguksa Temple and sedentary image of Pirojana Buddha of the same temple; and statues of 12 animals excavated around the guard stone of the Tumulus of the King Minae.

The first outhouse displaying tumuluses is connected, with stairs, to the corridor between the rooms 6 and 7. The relics displayed are those excavated in Ch'ŏnmach'ong, the typical one-room stone-built tomb, Kŭmgwanch'ong, Tumulus of Kyodong, Kyerim Tumuluses, and Wolsŏngro Tumuluses, all the tumuluses of Kyŏngju.

Main relics are clay board on which flying horse is painted, golden crown, crown ornament, hat, belt, ear ring; iron, kettle, box, dish with curved legs made of bronze; horse equipments, weaponry, earthen ware, glass all excavated in Ch'ŏumach'ong, such accessories as golden crown, costumes, hat, belt; gilt bronze box, gilt bronze horn-like bowl; bronze ladle; roundheaded sword; some weapons; lidded dish; jar with handles, all excavated in Kŭmgwanch'ong; chest accessory, earring, necklace, green earthen ware, dish with curved legs, all found in Wolsŏngro Tumuluses; and ornamented sword, accessory with gilt goblin face, wheel-like earthern ware, damascening jade necklace, lucky animal-like earthern ware with the body of turtle and the head and legs of dragon, and jar with clay icon attached, all excavated in Kyerim Tumuluses.

The second outhouse Anapjigwan lies behind the main building. In this outhouse are displayed the relics excavated in Wolji (the old name of Anapji) which, according to the legend, the 30th king of Shilla, Munmuwang, constructed after he conquered Paekje and Koguryŏ and he raised rare birds and animals here.

The relics excavated comprise such metallic artefacts as bronze dish, bronze spoon, gilt bronze scissors to cut the wick of lamp, gilt bronze crown, ring door handle with gilt bronze goblin face pattern attached, gilt bronze Chinese phoenix ornament, gilt bronze ornament mirror, and an ornamental hairpin; such Buddha images as gilt bronze Amitabha, gilt bronze, standing Buddha-to-be, god-general statue, and supplementary ornament; such wooden work as railing, lean-to, ancon, capital, rafter, ship, oar, penis, and an image of person; such lacquering works as picnic box, cup; such stationery as brazier, lampoil container, letter-engraved earthen ware, and inkstone; such earthen ware as painted bowl; such iron works as harpoon, plough, plowshare, ax, scissors, small knife, leaded round board, key and lock, and helmet; such tile and brick works as both concave and convex tiles, bricks, tile of devil face, broken bricks of famous writing.

In the garden of the museum, about two hundred stone relics transferred from the sites of temples and palaces are displayed. Most of these relics are stone statue of Buddha, stone pagoda, stone basin, stone lamp, monument base and these are surrounding the main building.

To the left from the museum, there is a bell in a bell house, a bell called Sŏngdŏkdaewang-shinjong which the 35th king of Unified Shilla, Kyŏngdŏkwang, to pray for the happiness of his dead father, began to make, only to be completed in the reign of the next king, Hyegong.

At first, this bell was placed at Pongdŏksa temple and transferred to Yŏngmyosa temple, to Nammun (South Gate) of Ŭpsŏng, to the old museum in Tongbu-dong, and finally to this present place in July 1975

On this bell, 4 flying images and 1037 letters are carved: "Marvelous work is completed. Its image is like a "mountain, its sound like the voice of dragon reaching canopy in the above and zenith at the bottom enough to make viewers feel awe and receive bliss". Also engraved are the names of the maker and the writer of letters.

① ②

① STANDING BHAISAJYAGURU gilt-bronze — Treasure No. 28
From Paengyul-sa Temple, Kyŏngju, Unified Shilla, A.D. 9th c. 179.0cm (H)

② DAGGER with ornamental sheath — Treasure No. 635.
Gold & Jade from District of King Mich'u Tumulus, Kyŏngju Old Shilla A.D. 5th-6th c. 36.0cm (L)

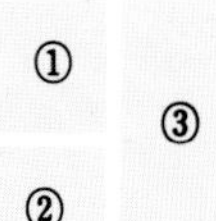

① MOUNTED WARRIOR WITH TWIN HORN CUPS
Stoneware probably from Doksan-ri, Kimhae
Three Kingdoms (Kaya) 5th C. (H) 23.2㎝(Nat'l Treasure No. 275)

② ZODIACAL FIGURE-BOAR
steatite probably from Tomb of General Kim Yu-sin, Kyongju Unified silla 8th C. (H) 40.8㎝

③ CROWN
gold from Ch'onma-ch'ong Tumulus, Kyongju Silla 5th~6th C. (H) 32.5㎝(Nat'l Treasure No. 188)

① ② ③

① SEATED BUDDHA (MAITREYA) TRAID granite from Jangch'ang-gol valley of Mt.Nam-san, Kyongju Silla 7th C. (H) 160.0cm(Buddha)

② HORSE & TIGER-SHAPED BUKLES bronze from O-un-dong, Yongch'on Early Iron Age early 1st C. (L) 22.4cm(Below)

③ FURNACE stoneware from Anap-chi Pond, Kyongju Unified Silla 8th C. (D) 30.2cm, (H) 19.5cm

Mystery ell of the King Sŏngdŏk

– Nat'l Treasure No. 29

① Mystery Bell of the King Sŏngdŏk under the dusk of evening.

② Flying Images.

Sŏngdŏkdaewang-shinjong, called Emile-jong, permeated with the regret of a child.

Then, the tension hang over. Several failures to make an excellent bell to pray for the happiness of the father, Songdŏkdaewang and the mother, Sodŏkdaehu was followed by the last attempt, in the pious belief and sincerity, at striking a bell. It was a very important occasion.

Many eyes of the people, including the 35th king of Shilla Kyŏngdŏkwang and courtiers, were centered on the person in charge of tolling the bell at noon. The time comes, then he tolls the bell.

Kwang –

The bell tolled but the sound was not what the king wanted, but that of crack and disappointment. Kyŏngdŏkwang died in the discouragement at the failure to make what he wanted and was followed by Hyegongwang, then 8. The new king's mother, Manwolbuin, reminded him of the bitter feelings of his father resulting from the disappointment.

It is natural posterity accomplish what the ancestor wanted to but could not.

In his strong willpower to make an unprecedented bell, the new king called in two ministes Kim, Ong and Kim, Yang-sang to order them to make a bell.

The two ministers in charge of making the bell had artisans make the mould of a bell and carve flying images. So, the last step of pouring melted iron remained. But the worry of failure made them hesitate to take the last step.

At that time, a strange rumor got around

"To make a mysterious bell, it is necessary to sacrifice an ignorant and untainted child by pouring it into the simmering iron liquid."

"Who would sacrifice his/her child?"

"But, it is necessary to make a mysteirous bell."

Kim, Ung and Kim, Yang-sang, after long thought, decided to fulfil the rumor getting around, but how they could do was a big problem.

They, in the hope that monks would give them a solution, came to convene many great monks across the country.

But any proper conclusion was not found, in a heated argument. Then, a friar going about asking for alms for the making of a mysterious bell said "Going about several villages, I visited a house a mother and a daughter lived in. I asked for alms, but the mother said, we are very poor not to give alms except for this child, so if you want, take it" and the mother soothed the child. The image was very affectionate, so I prayed for them. Now, as things go, what do you think of sacrificing the child?"

So, some courtiers and monks visited the house and asked for the alms. But the mother objected to the proposal by saying that she had said to the monk jokingly. But they took the child away from the mother by saying that we should not deceive Buddha and poured the child into simmering iron liquid.

The cry of the child echoing all over the world stopped and they poured iron liquid into the mould of the bell. Then, a perfect body of the bell was made.

At last, the day of tolling the bell came and all in the capital caught their breath and even the wind stopped blowing.

As the bell tolled, a soft, clear, and pitiful sound echoed, "Emile – "

The mysterious bell all national wanted and prayed for was finally completed.

Relics and vestiges connecting historical vein

A millennium has passed since the brilliant Shilla perished. Though relentless years flowed and myriads of temples and numberless pagodas crumbled, extant historic sites and relics which are scattered all over Kyŏngju are enough to form an art history of a country.

Including castles and mountain fortress protecting capital, Ch'ŏmsŏngdae, the oldest astronomical observatory in the Orient, Sŏgbinggo, ice storehouse, Kyerim mixed with the birth legend of the 4th king, T'alhae etc. are lying here and there in Kyŏngju.

With deep-rooted history, Kyŏngju has shown much heritage, so, for historians it is a very precious material connecting historic vein and, for people in general it is a very important sight-seeing place. Despite the fact mentioned above, there are still many relics to be dug up and it is impossible to say how many more historic remains are intered.

▶Whole view of Panwolsŏng Castle.

▲ Wolsŏng Castle, Kyŏngju — Historic Site No. 16

Located in Inwang-dong, Kyŏngju, this castle site is the place of a castle made of soil and stone. Its circumference is 2,400m, length 900m, width 260m, and area 198,000m². According to Samguksaki, this castle was built in A.D. 101 (22nd year of the King P'asa reign) and its distance was 1,423 feet. East, west, and north of castle have the ground hardened by stone and soil on which clay is covered on the contrary, south of the castle is in itself a cliff. This castle was used as the palace of kings and, as the country developed, the vicinity was annexed. Especially in the rule of the King Munmu, Anapchi, Imhaechŏn, and Ch'ŏmsŏngdae Observatory areas were annexed to the castle site, to make this site the very center of Shilla. And, for its crescent form, it is called Panwolsŏng castle or Shinwolsŏng castle. Also it is called Chaesŏng castle because king stayed here. This castle is very large and its natural environment was very beautiful. This area has the legend that Sŏk, T'al-hae took this place owned by Hogong, by cheat.

◀ Stone Icehouse — Treasure No. 66.

Located in Wolsŏng Castle, the icehouse, about 12.27m long, 5.76m wide and 5.21m high, is known as the storehouse for ice used during Chosŏn Dynasty. Though the details of construction are not known, the first record of this icehouse is connected with the King Yuri according to Samgukyusa, and ice was stored in the 6th year (A.D. 505) of the reign of the King Chijŭng.

The extant icehouse was, according to the monument for it, changed into stone icehouse from wooden one by Cho, Myŏng-gyŏm, then ruler of this area. On the cornerstone at the entrance is engraved the writing that ''Moved to current place after 4 years''. Stone icehouses built by the King Yŏngjo are extant in several places, this is preserved best.

▼ Ch'ŏmsŏngdae Observatory — Nat'l Treasure No. 31

Used in Shilla period to observe astronomical phenomenon, this is the oldest observatory in the Orient, and according to the record of separate note, Ki-i volume 2, Samgukyusa, "Ch'ŏmsŏngdae Observatory was made of processed stones", it is clear it was built during the reign of the Queen Sŏndŏk (A.D. 632-647) of Shilla. Under the supervision of Sŏk, O-won, the 16th generation posterity of the King T'alhae, this observatory was completed. Its material is granite and its structure can be divided into three parts; pedestal, cylindrical body, and sharp-shaped top.

The pedestal has two layers of square stones. Its southern facade is at an angle of 19 from due south. The cylindrical body is accumulated with 30cm-high fan-shaped stones 27 times. The height of 27 layers is 8.08m, the circumference of the lowest base, 16m, that of the 14th layer, 11.7m, that of the 27th layer, 9.2m. A square window with 95cm of each side is made from 13th layer to 15th layer in an angle of 16° from due east.

The inside bottom of the window is filled with stones of all sizes; the top is empty. On the 27th cylindrical body lie 4 two-layer sharp-shaped stones. This observatory is made of processed granite. The total number of stones is 365, which is flexible according as the pedestal stones are included or not.

It is said that three ladders were used to ascend the observatory.

▼ Kyerim Forest — Historic Site No. 19.

With the area of 7,300m^2, this forest dates back to the foundation of Shilla. It is thickly covered with zelkova trees, ash trees, and bush clovers. At first, it was called Shirim Forest and after Kim, Al-ji was born here, its name was changed into Kyerim Forest, which itself became the country name. In A.D. 65 (9th year of the King T'alhae). The King heard crow of rooster in one night from the western forest and he dispatched a servant to look all around. When he arrived there, a small shining box is suspended on a bough and a rooster is crowing under the bough. Being told of the story, the king sent for the box. When the box was opened, a bright-faced boy appeared.

Delighted he decided to bring him up. As the child grew up, he was very bright and intelligent. He was named Al-ji and his surname became Kim, because he came out of the golden box (Kim means gold). Also, the name of the forest was changed into Kyerim from Shirim, and Kyerim became the country name.

Stone Brick Pagoda of Punhwangsa Temple. — Nat'l Treasure No. 30

This pagoda is thought of as having been built when the Punhwangsa Temple — famous Shilla temple where such great monks as Chajang and Wonhyo stayed — was constructed in A.D. 634, the 3rd year of the Queen Sŏndŏk. It is made of processed andesite. On the 1-m high stone pedestal lie stone lion and stone seal on each edge. At its center, the body of the pagoda is accumulated. Though it is estimated that the pagoda was originally nine-storied, which is suspected considering the ratio of the formation of three stories. At the 4th side of the first story lies an entrance, both sides of which are engraved the statue of Deva king.

▶ **Hwangryongsa Temple Site** — Historic Site No. 6

First constructed in A.D. 513 (the 14th year of the 24th king of Shilla, Chinhŭng) and completed after 90 years, Hwangryongsa Temple was burned up during the Mongol Invasion. Judging from the remaining foundation stones on the field from Anapchi to Punhwangsa Temple, it is able to guess how big the temple was. Originally intended to be the place of a palace, it was changed into temple after brown dragon appeared in the hope that the dragon defend the country. It is said that there were Changyukchonbul and Nine-storied Pagoda, two of the Shilla's three treasures, and Kŭmdangpyŏkwa (Kŭmdang Mural painting) and the largest bell of the world in this temple.

① ②

① Thirteenth Story Stone Pagoda at Chŏnghyesa Temple Site
– Nat'l Treasure No. 40

Of many multi-storied stone pagodas of Shilla period, this papgoda has peculiar form unprecedented in the past. Its material is granite. Extant in the ruined Chŏnghyesa Temple Site, Oksan-ri, Angang-eŭb, Wolsŏng-gun, it is estimated to have been built in the period of Unified Shilla.

To support the body of pagoda, double pedestal consisting of 4 stones is laid. On each edge is raised stone column, on which four-storied lid stone lies. Then, the main body of the pagoda is gradually accumulated.

② Three-Storied Stone Pagoda as Kuhwang-ri – Nat'l Treasure No. 37

Typical three-storied stone pagoda built on two-storied pedestal, this pagoda is also called Hwangboksa Temple Site stone pagoda, because legend has it that it is located in temple of that name.

With the height of 7.3m, this pagoda reflects the change in architectural form of early unified Shilla: unlike the early stone pagoda which is structured with accumulated small stones, this uses one stone for pedestal and the number of small columns in pedestal decreased to two from three.

In 1942, when repair work was under way, gilt bronze box for containing bones of Buddha engraved with writing, two gold statues of Buddha, and many accessories were found. According to the writing, this pagoda was constructed somewhere between A.D. 692 (1st year of the King Hyoso) and 706 (5th year of the King Sŏngdŏk).

◀ East and West Three-Storied Stone Pagoda at Kamŭnsa Temple Site – Nat'l Treasure No. 112

It is said that Kamŭnsa Temple was built by the 31st king of Shilla, Shinmun who, following the will of his late father King Munmu, buried the body underwater. He built it to pray for the happiness of his father in the world beyond, and all the building included to the temple perished except for these two pagodas. Located in Yongdang-ri, Yangbuk-myŏn, Wolsŏng-gun, it has plane pedestal made of 12 stones.

The top pedestal consists of 12 plane stones and 8 lid stones, and the number of small columns between stores is 3 in bottom pedestal and 2 in top pedestal. The top part only has rectangular stone on three-storied lid stone and on the stone stands iron column alone. (Height: 13.4m)

Anapchi Lake and Limhaechŏn Palace Site-Historic Site No. 18.

Known as the reception hall or conference hall of ministers or the residence of the prince, this was constructed in A.D. 674 (14th year of the King Munmu), according to the record. Also says Samguksaki, in the 19th year of the King Munmu, palace was reconstructed magnificently and Limhaechŏn Palace Site was repaired in the 5th year of the King Aejang, 9th year of King Munsŏng, and 7th year of King Kyŏngmun. In this site, banquets for ministers were held in Sept. 6th year of the King Hyoso, March, 5th year of King Hyegong, Sept. 4th year of King Hŏnan, and March 7th year of King Hŏngang. After the King Kyŏngsun experienced the uproar of Kyŏnhwon, he invited Wanggŏn in 931 to appeal serious situation, so though it is an annexed palace, it was thought to be very important one.

According to a legend, this lake was made by digging, accumulating stones, and making mountain, in the imitation of Musan 12 Peaks (a Chinese mountain in the east of Sach'ŏn Province with 12 peaks on the top). In the middle of the lake, three islets (symbolizing the Taoist hermit's mountains underwater) were made with plants, flowers and rare birds and animals living there, according to the record.

Many relics including earthenware were excavated here and the Garden Lake of Shilla palace was restored during the clean-up work in 1980. Consulting the remaining wooden part found during the excavation work and other relics, three buildings were restored. Other building sites can be guessed by the cornerstones arranged in the original place.

①ORNAMENTAL STRIPS bone from Anap-chi Pond, Kyongju Unified Silla 8th~9th C. (L) 21.8㎝(Below)

②SPOONS bronze from Anap-chi Pond, Kyongju Unified Silla 8th~9th C. (L) 26.7㎝(Upper)

③STIRRUPS lacquered bronze probably from Hwang-o-dong, Kyongju Unified Silla 7th~8th C. (H) 14.7㎝(Left) (Treasure No. 1151)

④BOWL WITH INK SCRIPT stoneware from Anap-chi Pond, Kyongju Unified Silla 8th~9th C. (D) 11.3㎝ (H) 5.0㎝

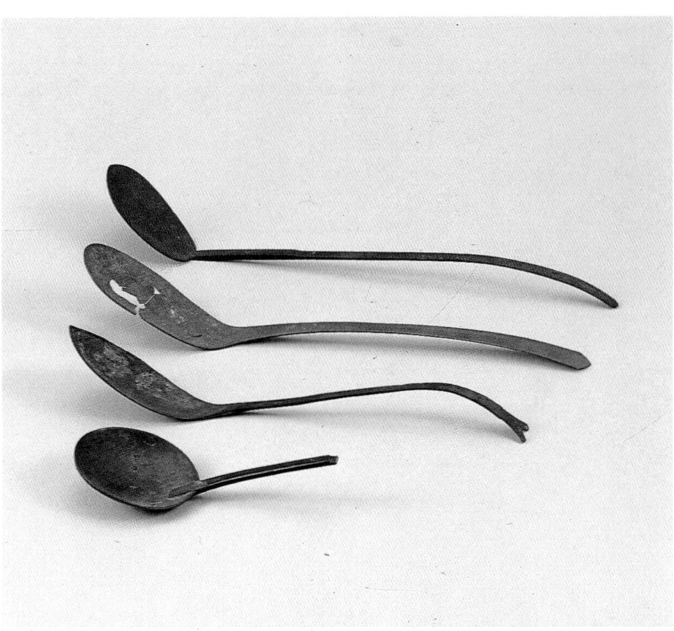

Pomun Tourism Complex Comprehensive tourism resort place, supplies various room for rest.

Pomun Tourism Complex is, by the Kyŏngju Tourism Comprehensive Development Plan, constructed on the area of about 3 million p'yŏng, centered on Pomun Lake, with accommodation, tourist center (conference hall), boat wharf, golf link, aquarium, Dot'urak World including playing facilities, shopping mall and subsidiary facilities. This complex which may be called comprehensive tourism place has the elegance and warmth of Kyŏngju area, the capital of Shilla matched with modern technology, so it can be called terrestrial paradise.

▼Whole view of Pomun Tourism Complex, spread beautifully in harmony of archaism and modernity.

① Distant view of Pomun Tourism Complex harmonized with blue waves.

② Night Guide Plan at the entrance to Pomun Tourism Complex.

보문관광휴양지

어서오십시오

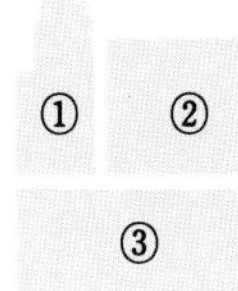

① Water Mill, reviving an aspect of old agricultural life.
② Tourism Monument under the dust of evening.
③ Night view of Pomun Tourism Complex.

62

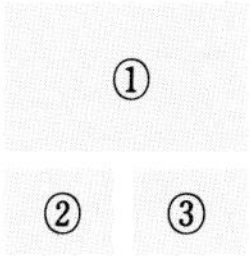

①	
②	③

① Convenience Facilities at Dot'urak World.
② Cruise of the ship "Swan", giving full sentiment of Pomun Lake.
③ Souvenir shops in harmony with Tourism Monument.

Shilla Culture Festival, revival of Brillant Shilla's tradition Culture

Biennially, in early October, Shilla Culture Festival is held at Kyŏngju, the capital during the millennium of Shilla, continuing for three days. Held at historic sites of Shilla and downtown Kyŏngju, this festival which is carried on by the people living in Kyŏngju and tourists revives the brilliancy of Shilla's traditional culture.

▼ Warfare Play-Important Intangible Cultural Assets No. 24

▶ Small Symbals Dance a kind of Buddhist dance, showing ecstasy of sublimating the human agony and pain into happiness and nirvana.

Kyŏngju Important Folk Culture Annual Event List

Month	Date	Name of Event	Contents of Event
2	Middle of the month	Ritual Sŏaksŏwon	Ritual cherishing the memory of three wise men of Shilla: Kim, Yu-shin, Ch'oi, Ch'i-won, and Sŏl, Ch'ong.
3	c. 20th	Ritual Samchŏnhyang	Ritual cherishing the memory of founding fathers of the families of Park, Kim, and Sŏk
	Middle	Ritual P'yoam	Ritual for the forefather of Kyŏngju Lee family
	25th in lunar calendar	Ritual Kŭmsan	Ritual for the general Kim, Yu-shin
	29th in lunar calendar	Ritual Wonhyodaesa	Ritual for the great monk Wonhyo
4	16th in lunar calendar	Ritual Koun	Ritual for the scholar Ch'oi, Ch'i-won
	8th in lunar calendar	Birthday of Buddha	Buddhist service, Rounding around Pagoda Lantern parade service in Sŏkkuram
8	7th in lunar calendar	Ritual Yukpuch'onjang	Ritual cherishing the memory of six chiefs of as many villages
9	20th of the month	Ritual Samchŏnhyang	Ritual cherishing the memory of founding fathers of the families of Park, Kim, and Sŏk
	25th in lunar calendar	Ritual Kŭmsan	Ritual for the general Kim, Yu-shin
10	8th-10th	Festival for Shilla Culture	Ritual of Unification, Sŏche, Parade, Folk Play, Buddhism event, Hangŭl composition competition. Korean Traditional Music Competition, Bonfire Play, Shilla Art Exhibition Academic Presentation Meeting
	Middle of the month	Citizens Athletic Meet	Citizens Athletic Meet and Folk Ssirŭm competition
11	Middle of the month	Citizens Amusement Performance	Folk dance, Folk Music Play etc.

List of Nationally Appointed Cultural Assets in Kyŏngju Area

① Tumulus and Related Relics.

Name	Location	Classification	Number
Monument of the Tumulus for the Shilla King T'aejongmuyŏl	Sŏak-dong	Nat'l Treasure	25
Golden Crown from Ch'ŏnmach'ong	Nat'l Kyŏngju Museum	Nat'l Treasure	188
Golden Hat from Ch'ŏnmach'ong	Nat'l Kyŏngju Museum	Nat'l Treasure	189
Golden Belt and Kwadae Ch'ŏnmach'ong	Nat'l Kyŏngju Museum	Nat'l Treasure	190
Golden Crown and Ornament (Northern Tumulus, No. 98)	Nat'l Kyŏngju Museum	Nat'l Treasure	191
Golden Belt and Kwadae (Northern Tumulus, No. 98)	Nat'l Kyŏngju Museum	Nat'l Treasure	192
Glass Bottle and Grail (Southern Tumulus, No. 98)	Nat'l Kyŏngju Museum	Nat'l Treasure	193
Golden Ornament (Southern Tumulus, No. 98)	Nat'l Kyŏngju Museum	Nat'l Treasure	194
Lidded Grail with figurine ornament (King Mich'u Tumulus)	Nat'l Kyŏngju Museum	Nat'l Treasure	195
Turtle-shaped pedestal, Sŏak-ri Kyŏngju	Sŏak-dong	Treasure	70
Golden Butterfly Ornament for Crown from Ch'ŏnmach'ong	Nat'l Kyŏngju Museum	Treasure	617
Golden Birdwing-shaped ornament for crown from Ch'ŏnmach'ong	Nat'l Kyŏngju Museum	Treasure	618
Kyŏngsik ornament from Ch'ŏnmach'ong	Nat'l Kyŏngju Museum	Treasure	619
Glass Grail from Ch'ŏnmach'ong	Nat'l Kyŏngju Museum	Treasure	620
Gilt bronze Sword with round grip and Chinese phoenix ornament from Ch'ŏnmach'ong	Nat'l Kyŏngju Museum	Treasure	621
Gilt bronze Ch'odu from Ch'ŏnmach'ong	Nat'l Kyŏngju Museum	Treasure	622
Golden Hun and Ring (Northern Tumulus, No. 98)	Nat'l Kyŏngju Museum	Treasure	623
Silver Kyŏnggab (Northern Tumulus, No. 98)	Nat'l Kyŏngju Museum	Treasure	632
Golden Sword with damascening	Nat'l Kyŏngju Museum	Treasure	635
Tumulus for the King Muyŏl	Sŏak-dong	Historic Site	20
Tumulus for Kim, Yu-shin	Ch'unghyo-dong	Historic Site	21
Square Tumulus, Kuojŏn-ri, Kyŏngju	Kujŏng-dong	Historic Site	27
Tumulus for the King Sŏngdŏk	Choyang-dong	Historic Site	28
Tumulus for the King Hŏndŏk	Tongch'ŏn-dong	Historic Site	29
Group of Tumuluses, Tong-ri, Kyŏngjuro Road	Nodong-dong	Historic Site	38
Group of Tumuluses, Sŏ-ri Kyŏngjuro Road	Nosŏ-dong	Historic Site	39
Group of Tumuluses, Hwangnam-ri Kyŏngju	Hwangnam-dong	Historic Site	40
Group of Tumuluses, Hwango-ri, Kyŏngju	Hwango-dong	Historic Site	41
Group of Tumuluses, Inwang-ri, Kyŏngju	Inwang-dong	Historic Site	42
Group of Tumuluses, Sŏak-ri Kyŏngju	Sŏak-dong	Historic Site	142
Eastern Historic Area, Kyŏngju	Hwangnam-dong	Historic Site	161
Five Tumuluses of Shilla	T'ap-dong	Historic Site	172
Tumulus for the King Ilsŏng	T'ap-dong	Historic Site	173
Tumulus for the King T'alhae	Tongch'ŏn-dong	Historic Site	174
Tumulus for the King Mich'u	Hwangnam-dong	Historic Site	175
Tumulus for the King Pŏpŭng	Hyohyŏn-dong	Historic Site	176
Tumulus for the King Chinhŭng	Sŏak-dong	Historic Site	177
Tumulus for the King Chinji and Munsŏng	Sŏak-dong	Historic Site	178
Tumulus for the King Hŏnan	Sŏak-dong	Historic Site	179
Tumulus for the King Chinp'yŏng	Pomun-dong	Historic Site	180
Tumulus for the King Shinmun	Paeban-dong	Historic Site	181
Tumulus for the Queen Sŏndŏk	Pomun-dong	Historic Site	182
Tumulus for the King Hyogong	Paeban-dong	Historic Site	183
Tumulus for the King Hyoso	Choyang-dong	Historic Site	184
Tumulus for the King Shinmu	Tongbang-dong	Historic Site	185
Tumulus for the King Chŏnggang	Namsan-dong	Historic Site	186
Tumulus for the King Hŏngang	Namsan-dong	Historic Site	187
Tumulus for the King Naemul	Kyo-dong	Historic Site	188
Tumulus for the King Paeri	Pae-dong	Historic Site	219
Tumulus for the King Sami	Pae-dong	Historic Site	221
Tumulus for the King Kyŏngae	Pae-dong	Historic Site	222
Tumulus for the King Kyŏngjugan	Hwango-dong	Kyŏngsang-buk-do Monument	31
Tumulus for the King Kim, In-mun	Sŏak-dong	Kyŏngsang-buk-do Monument	32
Tumulus for the King Kim, Yang	Sŏak-dong	Kyŏngsang-buk-do Monument	33
Site of Kyŏngju Nŭngji Pagoda	Paeban-dong	Kyŏngsang-buk-do Monument	34

② Buddhism Cultural Assets.

Name	Location	Classification	Number
Precinct of Pulguksa Temple	Chinhyŏn-dong	Historic Site and Scenic Beauty	1
Tabot'ap at Pulguksa Temple	Chinhyŏn-dong	Historic Site and Scenic Beauty	20
Three-story stone pagoda at Pulguksa Temple	Chinhyŏn-dong	Historic Site and Scenic Beauty	21
Yonhwagyo Bridge and Ch'ilbogyo Bridge at Pulguksa Temple	Chinhyŏn-dong	Historic Site and Scenic Beauty	22
Ch'ŏngungyo Bridge and Paegnagyo Bridge at Pulguksa Temple	Chinhyŏn-dong	Historic Site and Scenic Beauty	23
Stone cave of Sŏkkuram	Chinhyŏn-dong	Historic Site and Scenic Beauty	24
Gilt bronze sedentary statue of Pirojanabul at Pulguksa Temple	Chinhyŏn-dong	Historic Site and Scenic Beauty	26
Gilt bronze sedentary statue of Amitabha at Pulguksa Temple	Chinhyŏn-dong	Historic Site and Scenic Beauty	27
Gilt bronze standing statue Yaksayŏrae at Paigryulsa Temple	Nat'l Kyŏngju Museum	Historic Site and Scenic Beauty	28
Mystery Bell of the King Sŏngdŏk	Nat'l Kyŏngju Museum	Historic Site and Scenic Beauty	29
Stone Pagoda at Punhwangsa Temple	Kuhwang-dong	Historic Site and Scenic Beauty	30
Three-story stone pagoda, Kuhwang-ri Kyŏngju	Kuhwang-dong	Historic Site and Scenic Beauty	37
Three-story stone pagoda, at Kosŏnsa Temple Site	Nat'l Kyŏngju Museum	Historic Site and Scenic Beauty	38
Relics found in the Three-story stone pagoda, Pulguksa Temple	Nat'l Gentral Museum	Historic Site and Scenic Beauty	126